Longman
Practice Tests
for the TOEFL®

Deborah Phillips

Longman

Longman Practice Tests for the TOEFL

Longman Group UK Ltd
Longman House, Burnt Mill, Harlow,
Essex CM20 2JE, England
And Associated Companies throughout the world.

First published 1989
Tenth impression 1995

Published in the United States of America by
Longman Publishing, The Longman Building,
95 Church Street, White Plains,
New York 10601, U.S.A.

ISBN 0-582-03755-7

Executive editor: Joanne Dresner
Development editor: Marjorie Fuchs
Production editor: Elsa van Bergen
Text design: Jill Francis Wood
Cover design: Joseph De Pinho
Production supervisor: Judith Stern

Produced through Longman Malaysia, CL

CONTENTS

INTRODUCTION

ABOUT THIS BOOK

Purpose of the Book

This book is intended to prepare students for the TOEFL® (Test of English as a Foreign Language). It is based on the most up-to-date information available on the format and style of actual TOEFL tests.

Longman Practice Tests for the TOEFL® can be used in a variety of ways, depending on the needs of the reader.

1. It can be used in conjunction with *Longman Preparation Course for the TOEFL®* as the primary classroom texts in a course emphasizing TOEFL preparation.
2. It can be used as a supplementary text to provide TOEFL practice in a more general ESL course.
3. It can be used as a tool for individualized study by students preparing for the TOEFL outside of the ESL classroom.

What's In the Book

This book contains materials for the practice of test-taking strategies on TOEFL-format tests. The following are included:

1. **TOEFL Strategies** provides students with a plan for improving performance.
2. **Five TOEFL-format tests** allow students to practice the suggested strategies.
3. A **Listening Comprehension Tapescript** gives a transcription of the Listening Comprehension Section of each Practice Test.
4. **Answer Keys** include answers to all questions on the five Practice Tests.
5. **Scoring Information** allows students to determine approximate TOEFL scores on their Practice Tests.
6. **A Chart** allows students to record their progress on each of the Practice Tests.
7. **Answer Sheets,** beginning on page 167, allow students to practice correctly filling in the TOEFL forms.

Other Available Materials

1. *Longman Practice Tests for the TOEFL® Cassettes* contain recordings of the Listening Comprehension sections of each Practice Test.
2. *Longman Preparation Course for the TOEFL®* thoroughly prepares students for the TOEFL. Students learn specific strategies and develop skills for successfully answering each type of TOEFL question. TOEFL-format pre- and post-tests are included.
3. *Longman Preparation Course for the TOEFL® Cassettes* contain recordings of the Listening Comprehension section of the pre- and post-tests, and recordings of the Listening Comprehension exercises.
4. *Longman Preparation Course for the TOEFL®: Tapescript and Answer Key* contains the script for all recorded material and answers to all exercises. Answers for the Structure and Written Expression exercises include comments to help students understand the right answers.

ABOUT THE TOEFL

Description of the TOEFL

The Test of English as a Foreign Language (TOEFL) is a test to measure the level of English proficiency of non-native speakers of English. It is required primarily by English-language colleges and universities. Additionally, institutions such as government agencies or scholarship programs may require this test.

The test currently has the following sections:

1. **Listening Comprehension** (multiple choice): To demonstrate their ability to understand spoken English, examinees must listen to a tape and respond to various types of questions.
2. **Structure and Written Expression** (multiple choice): To demonstrate their ability to recognize grammatically correct English, examinees must choose the correct way to complete sentences and must find errors in sentences.
3. **Vocabulary and Reading Comprehension** (multiple choice): To demonstrate their ability to understand written English, examinees must answer vocabulary questions and must also answer questions about reading passages.
4. **Test of Written English** (written): Examinees must write an essay on a given topic in 30 minutes to demonstrate their ability to produce correct and meaningful English. The Test of Written English is given at certain times only.

The following chart outlines the probable format of a TOEFL test. It should be noted that on certain occasions a longer version of the TOEFL is given.

	TOEFL	TIME
LISTENING COMPREHENSION	50 questions	30 minutes*
STRUCTURE AND WRITTEN EXPRESSION	40 questions	25 minutes
VOCABULARY AND READING COMPREHENSION	60 questions	45 minutes
TEST OF WRITTEN ENGLISH	l essay question	30 minutes

*Approximate time.

What Your TOEFL Score Means

The TOEFL is scored on a scale of 200 to 700 points. There is no passing score on the TOEFL, but various institutions have their own TOEFL score requirements. You must find out from each institution what TOEFL score is required.

When you take the Practice TOEFL Tests in this book, it is possible for you to estimate your TOEFL score. A description of how to estimate your TOEFL score has been provided at the back of this book on pages 164 and 165.

The score of the Test of Written English is not included in your overall TOEFL score. It is a separate score on a scale of 1 to 6.

Where to Get Additional Information

Additional information is available in the *Bulletin of Information for TOEFL and TSE*. You can obtain this bulletin free of charge by sending a request to the following address:

Test of English as a Foreign Language
CN 6151
Princeton, NJ 08541-6151
U.S.A.

TO THE STUDENT

How to Prepare for the TOEFL

The TOEFL is a **test** of **English**. To do well on this test you should therefore work in two areas to improve your score:

1. You must work on improving your knowledge of the English language.
2. You must work on the skills and strategies specific to the TOEFL test.

When preparing for the TOEFL, it is important to work on TOEFL materials. However, work on TOEFL materials alone will not make you successful; a good basic knowledge of the English language is also necessary. Therefore, do not forget the general study of the English language as you prepare for the TOEFL.

How to Use This Book

1. When taking practice tests, try to reproduce the conditions of a real TOEFL.
    * Take each section of the test without interruption.
    * Work on only one section at a time.
    * Use the answer sheets from the back of this book.
    * Use a pencil to **completely** fill in the answer oval that corresponds to the answer you choose.
        Example:
    * Erase **completely** any changes you make on the answer sheet.
    * Time yourself for each test section. You need to experience the time pressure that exists on actual TOEFL tests.
    * Play the Listening Comprehension tape one time only during the test.
    * Mark only your answer sheet. You cannot write in a TOEFL test booklet.
2. Check your answers only at the end of each section or test. Do not check your answers after each question.
3. When you have completed a section or test and have checked your answers, compute your score (pages 164–165) and record the results on the chart (page 166). This chart will be a record of your progress as you work through the book.
4. After you compute your score, it is essential to review the answers carefully. The same types of questions appear again and again on the TOEFL. If you understand a mistake the first time you make it, you will probably get that same type of question correct on the following tests. This is how your TOEFL score will improve.
5. If you consistently miss certain types of questions, you should refer to specific exercises on those types of questions in the *Longman Preparation Course for the TOEFL®*.

TO THE TEACHER

How to Prepare for the Practice Tests

Before assigning the Practice Tests, you should be sure that the students have a clear idea of what sections and types of questions to expect on the TOEFL and of what strategies can be most effective in each of the sections. It can be most helpful to the students to discuss thoroughly the information in the introduction to this text, particularly the sections describing the TOEFL and the strategies for each section, before undertaking the Practice Tests.

How to Give the Practice Tests

It is esssential that the Practice Tests be taken under conditions as similar as possible to actual TOEFL conditions. (See the previous page.) Make sure the Listening Comprehension tapes are ready to be played. Show the students how to fill out the answer sheets; there is one complete set of forms for each Practice Test at the back of this book. Point out the Test of Written English, an additional 30-minute segment of certain TOEFLs.

How to Review the Practice Tests

Students can benefit tremendously from a thorough review of the Practice Tests. The following suggestions can help to make the Practice Test review sessions as effective as possible.

1. As you review the Practice Tests, be sure to discuss each answer—the incorrect answers as well as the correct answers. Discuss how students can determine that an answer is correct or incorrect.
2. As you review the Practice Tests, you should also reinforce how TOEFL strategies could have been used to determine correct and incorrect answers.
3. Two different methods are possible for reviewing the listening exercises. One way to review these exercises is to play back the tape, stopping after each question to discuss the skills and strategies involved in determining correct and incorrect answers. Another method is to have the students refer to the tape script at the back of the book to discuss each question.

TOEFL STRATEGIES
LISTENING COMPREHENSION

The first section of the TOEFL is the Listening Comprehension Section. It consists of 50 questions (some versions of the tests may be longer). You will listen to recorded material and respond to questions about the material. You must listen carefully, because you will hear the tape one time only, and the material on the tape is not written in your test booklet.

There are three types of questions in the Listening Comprehension Section of the TOEFL:

1. **Part A** (questions 1–20) consists of 20 sentences. You must choose, from the four choices in your test booklet, the sentence that is closest in meaning to the sentence you hear on the tape.
2. **Part B** (questions 21–35) consists of 15 short conversations, each followed by a question. You must choose the best answer to each question from the four choices in your test booklet.
3. **Part C** (questions 36–50) consists of longer conversations or talks, each followed by a number of questions. You must choose the best answer to each question from the four choices in your test booklet.

GENERAL STRATEGIES

1. **During the directions, look ahead at the answers.** The directions on every TOEFL are the same, so it is not necessary to listen carefully to them. You should be completely familiar with the directions before the day of the test. You can then use the time when the directions are being given to look ahead at the answers to any questions on the same page as the directions. (You may not look ahead at another page during the directions.)
2. **Listen carefully to the sentences, conversations, and short talks.** You should concentrate fully on what the speakers are saying in questions 1–50.
3. **Choose the best answer to each question.** You should guess even if you are not sure; never leave any answers blank. (There is no penalty for guessing on the TOEFL.)
4. **Use any remaining time to look ahead at the answers to the questions that follow.** When you finish with one question, you may have time to look ahead at the answers to the next question.

LISTENING COMPREHENSION—PART A

For each of the 20 questions in Part A of the Listening Comprehension Section of the TOEFL, you will hear a short sentence on tape. After you hear the sentence, you must choose from the test booklet the answer that is closest in meaning to the sentence you hear on the tape.

Example

You will hear: [Don read the book from cover to cover.]*

You will read: (A) Don read the cover of the book.
(B) Don read all of the book.
(C) Don put a cover on the book.
(D) Don was under the bed covers
        when he read the book.

Answer (B) is closest in meaning to the sentence you hear on the tape. The expression "from cover to cover" means "all of the book."

STRATEGIES FOR LISTENING COMPREHENSION—PART A

1. **During the directions for Listening Comprehension—Part A, look ahead at the answers to questions 1–20.** Look ahead at the questions that are on the same page as the directions. You may **not** turn the page during the directions.

2. **Listen carefully as the sentences in questions 1–20 are spoken.** As you listen to the sentences, remember the following:

   - Be careful of answers that sound similar to what you hear on the tape. They are usually not the correct ones.
   - Be careful of negatives. An idea expressed negatively on the tape may be expressed positively in the answers or vice versa.
   - Pay attention to the time (past, present, future) of the verb.
   - Pay attention to *who* is doing *what*.

3. **Choose the best answer to each question.** Remember to answer each question even if you are not sure of the correct response.

4. **Use any remaining time to look ahead at the answers to the questions that follow.**

---

*In this book, material that you would hear only on the tape is enclosed in brackets.

LISTENING COMPREHENSION—PART B

For each of the 15 questions in Part B of the Listening Comprehension Section of the TOEFL, you will hear a short conversation between two speakers followed by a question. After you listen to the conversation and the question, you must choose the best answer to the question from your test booklet.

Example

You will hear:
Man: [I've always wanted to visit Hawaii with you.
Woman: Why not next month?
Q: WHAT DOES THE WOMAN MEAN?]

You will read: (A) Next month isn't a good time for
                        the trip.
                   (B) She doesn't want to go to Hawaii.
                   (C) She suggests taking the trip next
                        month.
                   (D) She's curious about why he
                        doesn't want to to.

Answer (C) is the best answer to the question. "Why not next month?" is a suggestion that they take the trip next month.

STRATEGIES FOR LISTENING COMPREHENSION—PART B

1. **During the directions for Listening Comprehension—Part B, look ahead at the answers to questions 21–35.** Look ahead at the answers to the questions that are on the same page as the directions. You may **not** turn the page during the directions.

2. **Listen carefully as the conversations in questions 21–35 are spoken.** As you listen to the conversations, remember the following:

   - Be careful of answers that sound similar to what you hear on the tape. They are usually not the correct ones.
   - Be careful of negatives. An idea expressed negatively on the tape may be expressed positively in the answers or vice versa.
   - Listen carefully to the second line of conversation because it often contains the answer to the question.
   - Draw conclusions about *who, what,* and *where.*

3. **Choose the best answer to each question.** Remember to answer each question even if you are not sure of the correct response.

4. **Use any remaining time to look ahead at the answers to the questions that follow.**

LISTENING COMPREHENSION—PART C

Listening Comprehension—Part C consists of longer passages, each followed by a number of questions. You will hear the passages and the questions on a tape; they are not written in your test booklet. You must choose the best answer to each question from the four choices that are written in your test booklet.

Passages

The long passages in Listening Comprehension—Part C of the TOEFL may be in the form of either a conversation between two people or a talk by one. The conversations are often about some aspect of school life or about topics currently in the news in the United States.

The talks are most often lectures from university courses on subjects relating to the United States.

Questions and Answers

There are three very common kinds of questions about the passages in Listening Comprehension—Part C of the TOEFL.

1. **Main Idea, Subject, or Topic Questions**
   For almost every passage in Listening—Part C of the TOEFL, there is one main idea, subject or topic question. This question refers to the entire passage rather than just one detail. The following are examples of this type of question:

   - What is the topic of this talk?
   - What is the main idea of this passage?
   - What is the subject of this conversation?

2. **Inference Questions**
   It is very common to have an inference question about each passage in Listening—Part C of the TOEFL. An inference question is a question that is not answered directly in the passage; you must draw a conclusion from information given in the passage. (You have already used this type of skill in Listening—Part B.) The words "probably" and "most likely" indicate that a question is not answered directly in the passage. The following are examples of inference questions:

   - Where does this conversation *probably* take place?
   - Who is *most likely* giving this talk?
   - In what course would this talk *most likely* be given?

3. **Detail Questions**
   The majority of questions in Listening—Part C are detail questions. This means that the questions are answered directly in the passage. The following are examples of detail questions:

   - In what year did the action occur?
   - What caused him to act that way?
   - How did he find out that he was wrong?

There are two important ideas to remember when you are answering detail questions. First, **the detail questions are generally answered in order in the passage.** The first detail question is answered near the beginning of the passage, and the last detail question is answered near the end of the passage. Next, the answers in Listening—Part C do not always sound different from what you hear on the tape. Remember that the correct answers in Listening—Part A and Listening—Part B very often *sound different* from what is said on the tape. In Listening—Part C this is not true. **The answers in Part C very often sound the same as what is said on the tape.** Sometimes, however, the correct answer sounds different from what is said on the tape.

STRATEGIES FOR LISTENING COMPREHENSION—PART C

1. **During the directions to Listening Comprehension—Part C, look ahead at the answers to questions 36–50.** Look ahead at the answers to questions that are on the same page as the directions. You may **not** turn the page during the directions. While you are looking ahead at the answers, you should try to do the following:

   - Anticipate the **topics** of the passages you will hear.
   - Anticipate the **questions** for each of the groups of answers.

2. **Listen carefully to the first line of the passage.** It often contains the main idea, subject, or topic of the passage.

3. **As you listen to the passage, draw conclusions about who is talking and where the talk or conversation takes place.** You will often be asked to make such inferences in the questions about the passage.

4. **As you listen to the passage, follow along with the answers in your test booklet, and try to determine the correct answers.** Detail questions are generally answered in order in the passage, and the answers often sound the same as what is said on the tape.

5. **You should guess even if you are not sure;** never leave any answers blank.

6. **Use any remaining time to look ahead at the answers to the questions that follow.**

STRUCTURE AND WRITTEN EXPRESSION

The second section of the TOEFL is the Structure and Written Expression Section. This section consists of 40 questions (some versions of the tests may be longer). You have 25 minutes to complete the 40 questions in this section.

There are two types of questions in the Structure and Written Expression Section of the TOEFL:

1. **Structure** (questions 1–15) consists of 15 sentences in which part has been replaced with a blank. Each sentence is followed by four answer choices. You must choose the answer that completes the sentence in a grammatically correct way.
2. **Written Expression** (questions 16–40) consists of 25 sentences in which four words or groups of words have been underlined. You must choose the underlined word or group of words that is **not** correct.

GENERAL STRATEGIES

1. **Make the best use of your time.** Because you must complete 40 questions in 25 minutes (on a standard test), you have only slightly more than 30 seconds per question. You must therefore work quickly and efficiently through this section of the test.
2. **Begin with questions 1 through 15.** Anticipate that questions 1 through 5 will be rather easy. Anticipate that questions 11 through 15 will be rather difficult. Do not spend too much time on questions 11 through 15. There will be easier questions that come later.
3. **Continue with questions 16 through 40.** Anticipate that questions 16 through 20 will be rather easy. Anticipate that questions 36 through 40 will be rather difficult. Do not spend too much time on questions 36 through 40.
4. **If you have time, return to questions 11 through 15.** You should spend extra time on questions 11 through 15 only after you spend all the time you want on the other easier questions.
5. **Do not leave any questions blank on your answer sheet.** Even if a question is very difficult, you should answer the question. There is no penalty for guessing on the TOEFL.

STRUCTURE

Questions 1 through 15 test your knowledge of the correct structure of English sentences. They are multiple choice questions in which you must choose the letter of the answer that best completes the sentence.

Example

_____ is taking a trip to New York.

(A) They
(B) When
(C) The woman
(D) Her

In this example, you should notice immediately that the sentence has a verb ("is taking"), and that the verb needs a subject. Answers (B) and (D) are incorrect because "when" and "her" are not subjects. In answer (A) "they" is a subject, but "they" is plural, and the verb "is taking" is singular. The correct answer is (C); "the woman" can be a singular subject. You should therefore choose answer (C).

STRATEGIES FOR THE STRUCTURE QUESTIONS

1. **First study the sentence.** Your purpose is to determine what is needed to complete the sentence correctly.

2. **Then study each answer to determine how well it completes the sentence.** Eliminate answers that do not complete the sentence correctly.

3. **Do not try to eliminate incorrect answers by looking only at the answers.** The incorrect answers are generally correct by themselves. The incorrect answers are generally incorrect only when used to complete the sentence.

4. **Never leave any answers blank.** Be sure to answer each question even if you are unsure of the correct response.

5. **Do not spend too much time on the Structure questions.** Be sure to leave adequate time for the Written Expression questions.

WRITTEN EXPRESSION

Questions 16 through 40 test your knowledge of the correct way to express yourself in English writing. Each question in this section consists of one sentence in which four words or groups of words have been underlined. You must choose the letter of the word or group of words that is **not** correct.

Example

    The <u>final</u> delivery of <u>the day</u> <u>is</u> the <u>importantest</u>.
         A   B   C   D

If you look at the underlined words in this example, you should notice immediately that "importantest" is not correct. The correct superlative form of "important" is "the most important." Therefore, you should choose answer (D) because (D) is not correct.

Example

    The books <u>that</u> I <u>read</u> <u>was</u> <u>interesting</u>.
              A   B   C   D

If you look at the underlined words in this example, each word by itself appears to be correct. However, the singular verb "was" is incorrect because it does not agree with the plural subject "books." Therefore, you should choose answer (C) because (C) is not correct.

STRATEGIES FOR THE WRITTEN EXPRESSION QUESTIONS

1. **First look at each of the four underlined words or groups of words.** You want to see if you can spot which of the four answer choices is **not** correct.

2. **If you have been unable to find the error by looking only at the four underlined expressions, then read the complete sentence.** Some underlined expressions are incorrect because of something in another part of the sentence.

3. **Never leave any answers blank.** Be sure to answer each question even if you are unsure of the correct response.

VOCABULARY AND READING COMPREHENSION

The third section of the TOEFL is the Vocabulary and Reading Comprehension Section. This section consists of 60 questions (some versions of the tests may be longer). You have 45 minutes to complete the 60 questions in this section.

There are two types of questions in the Vocabulary and Reading Comprehension Section of the TOEFL:

1. **Vocabulary** (questions 1–30) consists of 30 sentences in which a word or group of words has been underlined. Each sentence is followed by four answer choices. You must choose the answer that is closest in meaning to the underlined word or group of words.
2. **Reading Comprehension** (questions 31–60) consists of five or six reading passages, each followed by a number of questions. The questions must be answered based upon what is stated or implied in the passages.

GENERAL STRATEGIES

It is up to you to decide how much of your time you will spend on vocabulary and how much on reading. The biggest mistake that students make in this section is to spend too much time on vocabulary (because it comes first) and not enough time on reading. Repeated experiments with students have demonstrated again and again that when students are given extra time to go over the Vocabulary section, they do not improve their scores; either they know the meaning of a word the first time they read a question or they do not.

However, when students are given extra time on the Reading Comprehension section, their scores do improve. Therefore, the most important message to students for the Vocabulary and Reading Comprehension Section of the TOEFL is to **complete the Vocabulary section quickly and efficiently and move directly on to the reading section. Use any extra time to go over the reading questions.**

1. **Begin with vocabulary questions 1–30.** Complete this section quickly and efficiently. You can do this by looking at the underlined word and the answers. You do not need to read the complete sentences carefully.
2. **Continue with reading comprehension questions 31–60.** Work slowly and carefully through the reading section.
3. **If you have any time remaining, then return to the vocabulary questions.** You should return to the vocabulary questions only if you have spent all the time that you need on the reading questions.
4. **Never leave any questions blank on your answer sheet.** Even if a question is very difficult and you are unsure of the correct response, you should answer the question.

VOCABULARY

Each vocabulary question consists of a sentence with an underlined word or group of words. This sentence is followed by four answer choices. You must choose the answer that is closest in meaning to the underlined word or group of words. You must also be sure not to change the meaning of the sentence.

Example

The earth is <u>divided</u> into two hemispheres.

(A) chopped
(B) joined
(C) separated
(D) mixed

Of the four answer choices, answer (C) "separated" is closest in meaning to the underlined word "divided." Also the sentence "The earth is separated into two hemispheres" has approximately the same meaning as "The earth is divided into two hemispheres." Therefore, answer (C) is the best answer.

STRATEGIES FOR THE VOCABULARY QUESTIONS

1. **Work quickly through the Vocabulary section.** The questions progress from easy to difficult. Do not spend too much time on the difficult questions.

2. **Do not look for grammatical clues to help you decide which vocabulary word goes in the blank.** The Vocabulary section does not test grammar.

3. **Do not spend a lot of time looking for contextual clues to the meanings of words.** The context usually doesn't help you understand the meaning of the word.

4. **Be careful of secondary meanings of words.** Words in English often have more than one meaning. The word "embrace," for example, has a primary meaning of "hug," but it can also mean "include." You must be aware that in the Vocabulary section of the TOEFL, the primary meaning of a word can be an incorrect answer and a secondary meaning of that word can be the correct answer.

5. **Never leave any answers blank.** Be sure to answer every question in the Vocabulary section even if you do not know the meanings of the words.

READING COMPREHENSION

The Reading Comprehension Section of the TOEFL consists of five or six reading passages, each followed by four to eight questions. Topics of the reading passages are varied, but they are often informational subjects that might be studied in an American university: American history, literature, art, architecture, geology, geography, and astronomy, for example.

STRATEGIES FOR THE READING PASSAGES

1. **Skim the reading passages to determine the main idea and the overall organization of ideas in the passage.** You do not need to understand every detail in each passage to answer the questions correctly. It is therefore a waste of time to read the passage with the intent of understanding every single detail before you try to answer the questions.

2. **Look ahead at the questions to determine what types of questions you must answer.** If you know the types of questions you must answer, you will know where to look in the passage to find the answers to the questions.

3. **Find the section of the passage that deals with each question.** If you understand the overall organization of ideas in the passage and you know what types of questions you must answer, you will know exactly where to look in the passage to find the correct answers. You can study the section of the passage that deals with each question thoroughly and carefully.

4. **Choose the best answer to each question from the four answer choices listed in your test booklet.** You can choose the best answer or answers according to what is given in the appropriate section of the passage, eliminate definitely wrong answers, and mark your best guess on the answer sheet.

THE TEST OF WRITTEN ENGLISH

The Test of Written English (TWE) is a writing section that appears on the TOEFL several times a year. If you are required to take the TWE, be sure to sign up for the TOEFL in one of the months that it is given.

On the TWE you will be given a specific question and you will be asked to answer that question in essay format in 30 minutes. The TWE will be given at the beginning of the TOEFL, before the Listening Comprehension, Structure and Written Expression, and Vocabulary and Reading Sections.

The TWE is currently emphasizing two different types of questions: (1) contrast questions and (2) interpretation of graphical data. In a contrast question you will be asked to discuss both sides of an issue and then indicate which position you agree with. In a graphical question you will be asked to interpret some type of graphical data and perhaps draw some conclusions about the data.

Because you must write a complete essay in such a short period of time, it is best for you to aim to write a basic, clear, concise, and well-organized essay. The following strategies should help you to write this type of essay:

GENERAL STRATEGIES

1. **Read the question carefully and answer the question exactly as it is asked.** Take several minutes at the beginning of the test to be sure that you understand the question and to outline a response that answers it.

2. **Organize your response very clearly.** You should think of having an introduction, body paragraphs that develop the introduction, and a conclusion to end your essay. Use transitions to help the reader understand the organization of ideas.

3. **Whenever you make any kind of general statement, be sure to support that idea with examples, reasons, facts, or similar details.**

4. **Stick to vocabulary and sentence structures that you know.** This is not the time to try out new words or structures.

5. **Finish writing your essay five minutes early so that you have time to proof what you wrote.**

PRACTICE TEST ONE

SECTION 1
LISTENING COMPREHENSION

In this section of the test, you will have an opportunity to demonstrate your ability to understand spoken English. There are three parts in this section, with special directions for each part.

Part A

Directions: For each question in Part A, you will hear a short sentence. Each sentence will be spoken just one time. The sentences you hear will not be written out for you. Therefore, you must listen carefully to understand what the speaker says.

After you hear a sentence, read the four choices in your test book, marked (A), (B), (C), and (D), and decide which <u>one</u> is closest in meaning to the sentence you heard. Then, on your answer sheet, find the number of the question and fill in the space that corresponds to the letter of the answer you have chosen. Fill in the space so the letter inside the oval cannot be seen.

Example I   Sample Answer

You will hear: ● Ⓑ Ⓒ Ⓓ

You will read: (A) John outran the others.
                 (B) John was the fastest hunter in
                       the chase.
                 (C) John wasn't the slowest in the
                       race.
                 (D) John was the last runner to
                       finish the race.

The speaker said, "John was the fastest runner in the race." Sentence (A), "John outran the others," is closest in meaning to the sentence you heard. Therefore, you should choose answer (A).

Example II   Sample Answer

You will hear: Ⓐ Ⓑ ● Ⓓ

You will read: (A) Could you help me use the rest?
                 (B) Do you mind using the other
                       desk?
                 (C) Would you mind helping me
                       carry this piece of furniture?
                 (D) If you move my desk, I'll help
                       you with your work.

The speaker said, "Could you help me move my desk?" Sentence (C), "Would you mind helping me carry this piece of furniture?" is closest in meaning to the sentence you heard. Therefore, you should choose answer (C).

GO ON TO THE NEXT PAGE

1. (A) Cars are dented whether or not it rains.
   (B) A lot of money is spent on cars in rainy weather.
   (C) Many traffic accidents occur in wet weather.
   (D) It will rain whether you take your car or not.

2. (A) Thomas will take his exams next week.
   (B) Thomas' exams last a week.
   (C) In the past week, the exams were postponed.
   (D) Thomas successfully completed his exams last week.

3. (A) The meeting was announced before I forgot.
   (B) I forgot to bring the announcement to the meeting.
   (C) The announcer forgot about the meeting.
   (D) I didn't tell them about the meeting.

4. (A) The book should be returned to the library within a week.
   (B) He isn't able to do his work in this book.
   (C) He's due for a raise this week.
   (D) The book was due last week.

5. (A) Sue took a vacation at Christmas time.
   (B) Sue spent her vacation time working in a store.
   (C) Sue went to several sales at Christmas time.
   (D) Sue's saleswoman took a vacation from work at Christmas time.

6. (A) Our grandparents have adjusted to San Francisco.
   (B) We saw our grandparents before we flew to San Francisco.
   (C) We took a plane trip to visit relatives.
   (D) Our grandparents flew to see us in San Francisco.

7. (A) I believe that the administration building is near the bookstore.
   (B) Is the bookstore in the administration building?
   (C) The administrators went next door to the bookstore.
   (D) Is the bookstore being built by the administration?

8. (A) The parking lots were full before 10:00.
   (B) It was impossible to start class by 10:00.
   (C) He parked the car before class at 10:00.
   (D) The possibility of finding a place to park was increased.

9. (A) Debbie shouldn't leave her purse here.
   (B) Debbie's probably in the apartment.
   (C) Debbie's purse must not be in the apartment.
   (D) Debbie left without taking her purse.

10. (A) She seems fond of the magazine.
    (B) She's lost the magazine.
    (C) The magazine seems to offend her.
    (D) She's been able to locate the magazine.

GO ON TO THE NEXT PAGE ➤

11. (A) Mary wrote the letter as directed.
    (B) The directions were given to Mary in a letter.
    (C) Mary followed the instructions in a letter.
    (D) Mary worked exactly as instructed.

12. (A) How did they invite you there for dinner?
    (B) Their dinner invitation was very kind.
    (C) The dinner was so nice.
    (D) Your dinner invitation was nicer than theirs.

13. (A) It's rare for me to work during my vacations.
    (B) I go on vacations whenever I can.
    (C) I almost never take a break from my job.
    (D) My vacations are rarely full of work.

14. (A) All the lawyer's preparation did no good.
    (B) The lawyer prepared nothing for the case.
    (C) It wasn't work for the lawyer to prepare for the case.
    (D) The lawyer didn't work to prepare for the case.

15. (A) The film wasn't very funny.
    (B) It was a rather boring movie.
    (C) He couldn't move any further.
    (D) The movie was extremely amusing.

16. (A) George must provide the class with paper this time.
    (B) George must turn in his paper to pass the class.
    (C) If George passes the class, he'll attend the summit.
    (D) If George submits to those people this time, he won't succeed.

17. (A) The bills should be paid immediately.
    (B) Waiting to pay the bills is important.
    (C) They mustn't pay the bills.
    (D) They must wait in line when they pay the bills.

18. (A) The university plans to recruit new athletes.
    (B) An area for sports will be constructed on campus.
    (C) The athletes felt that a new university should be planned.
    (D) They planned to meet at the building on the university athletic field.

19. (A) Paul turned to the board for a decision.
    (B) The board decided to turn Paul over to the authorities.
    (C) Paul was able to turn the decision over to the board.
    (D) The board's decision was reversed by Paul.

20. (A) He's pleased with his results.
    (B) He isn't satisfied with all his work.
    (C) He found that all his work wasn't satisfactory.
    (D) He satisfied all the panel with his findings.

GO ON TO THE NEXT PAGE

Part B

<u>Directions:</u>   In Part B you will hear short conversations between two speakers. At the end of each conversation, a third person will ask a question about what was said. You will hear each conversation and question about it just one time. Therefore, you must listen carefully to understand what each speaker says. After you hear a conversation and the question about it, read the four possible answers in your test book and decide which <u>one</u> is the best answer to the question you heard. Then, on your answer sheet, find the number of the question and fill in the space that corresponds to the letter of the answer you have chosen.

Look at the following example.

You will hear:

You will read: (A) The exam was really awful.
(B) It was the worst exam she had
ever seen.
(C) It couldn't have been more
difficult.
(D) It wasn't that hard.

<u>Sample Answer</u>

Ⓐ Ⓑ Ⓒ ●

From the conversation you learn that the man thought the exam was very difficult and that the woman disagreed with the man. The best answer to the question "What does the woman mean?" is (D), "It wasn't that hard." Therefore, you should choose answer (D).

21. (A) She paid more than the man.
(B) She had good fortune when she
bought the television.
(C) Fifty dollars is a fortune to her.
(D) Fifty dollars is too much to pay
for a television.

22. (A) A mathematician.
(B) A reporter.
(C) An accountant.
(D) An arithmetic teacher.

23. (A) At a sporting event.
(B) At the police station.
(C) In front of a movie theater.
(D) At a film developer's.

24. (A) She doesn't know how to type.
(B) She doesn't want to type
anymore.
(C) She hasn't typed the paper.
(D) She believes they're out of
paper.

25. (A) See the personnel manager
immediately.
(B) Wait for the personnel manager
to arrive.
(C) Arrange to meet with the
personnel manager the next
day.
(D) Break her appointment with the
personnel manager.

26. (A) She wants to be a school
playground leader.
(B) She's acting in a school theater
production.
(C) She's seen some students
rolling on the ground.
(D) Her new role is to lead the
school.

GO ON TO THE NEXT PAGE ➤

PRACTICE TEST ONE

27. (A) He doesn't want to live in an apartment.
    (B) He thought his signature was unnecessary.
    (C) His taste in apartments is different from theirs.
    (D) He doesn't always say what he means.

28. (A) Sally was quite early.
    (B) Sally was just barely on time.
    (C) Sally arrived a minute after they called her.
    (D) Sally arrived soon after the man.

29. (A) At a bus stop.
    (B) At a school.
    (C) In a dentist's office.
    (D) At a cleaning supplies store.

30. (A) She needs to have it back tomorrow.
    (B) She doesn't want her friend to borrow it.
    (C) She doesn't want to make any promises.
    (D) She doesn't think the sweater will fit.

31. (A) He's in his last week of work.
    (B) He doesn't expect the work to last.
    (C) The work isn't really hard.
    (D) He's only been working for a week.

32. (A) It was lucky that Tom wasn't injured in the accident.
    (B) Tom was a nervous wreck after the accident.
    (C) It was just an accident that Tom got a new car.
    (D) Tom wasn't very lucky.

33. (A) There's been nothing but snow for quite some time.
    (B) He's bored with the changing weather.
    (C) He believes that it'll snow in two weeks.
    (D) His friends think that he's boring when he talks about the weather.

34. (A) The man should order a history book immediately.
    (B) He can't get a text from the bookstore in time for the exam.
    (C) There are no more history texts on order at the bookstore.
    (D) His friend's using the history text during the exam.

35. (A) Listen to the symphony concert alone.
    (B) Stand on a long line.
    (C) Discuss a good idea of hers with the man.
    (D) Go to a concert tomorrow night.

Part C

Directions: In this part of the test, you will hear short talks and conversations. After each of them, you will be asked some questions. You will hear the talks and conversations and the questions about them just one time. They will not be written out for you. Therefore, you must listen carefully to understand what each speaker says.

After you hear a question, read the four possible answers in your test book and decide which one is the best answer to the question you heard. Then, on your answer sheet, find the number of the question and fill in the space that corresponds to the letter of the answer you have chosen.

GO ON TO THE NEXT PAGE ➤

Listen to this sample talk.

You will hear:

Now look at the following example.

You will hear: Sample Answer

You will read: (A) Art from America's inner cities.   Ⓐ Ⓑ Ⓒ ●
                (B) Art from the central region of
                    the U.S.
                (C) Art from various urban areas in
                    the U.S.
                (D) Art from rural sections of
                    America.

The best answer to the question "What style of painting is known as American regionalist?" is (D), "Art from rural sections of America." Therefore, you should choose answer (D).

Now look at the next example.

You will hear: Sample Answer

You will read: (A) *American Regionalist.*   Ⓐ Ⓑ ● Ⓓ
                (B) *The Family Farm in Iowa.*
                (C) *American Gothic.*
                (D) *A Serious Couple.*

The best answer to the question "What is the name of Wood's most successful painting?" is (C), "*American Gothic.*" Therefore, you should choose answer (C).

36. (A) Motivation.
    (B) Research for a management
        class.
    (C) Finding journal articles in the
        library.
    (D) The management professor.

37. (A) He can't decide on a topic.
    (B) He doesn't have too much time
        to complete the research.
    (C) He doesn't know where the
        library is.
    (D) He is uncertain how to find
        references.

38. (A) In an index.
    (B) In a journal.
    (C) In the card catalog.
    (D) In management class.

39. (A) Both books and journals.
    (B) Just references on motivation
        from the card catalog.
    (C) Only management and business
        books.
    (D) Journal articles only.

40. (A) A topic for his paper.
    (B) A research project.
    (C) A book on management.
    (D) An article on motivation.

GO ON TO THE NEXT PAGE ➤

PRACTICE TEST ONE

41. (A) Begin his research.
    (B) Go to management class.
    (C) Write a journal.
    (D) Look for a greeting card.

42 (A) United States History.
    (B) Famous Short Story Writers.
    (C) Survey of American Literature.
    (D) The Great American Novel.

43. (A) Edgar Allan Poe.
    (B) American poets.
    (C) The novel.
    (D) Short story writers.

44. (A) Short.
    (B) Symbolic.
    (C) Tragic.
    (D) Fulfilled.

45. (A) Symbolism.
    (B) Impressionism.
    (C) Eerie tone.
    (D) Humor.

46. (A) Read about Poe's life.
    (B) Prepare for a discussion of a short story.
    (C) Study the American novelist.
    (D) Write an analysis of one of the stories.

47. (A) A spoken language.
    (B) A written language.
    (C) A language based on road signs.
    (D) A language based on hand movements.

48. (A) The Indians didn't have spoken languages.
    (B) The Indians spoke many different languages.
    (C) The Indians were unable to use their mouths to speak.
    (D) Sign language is much more advanced than spoken language.

49. (A) Frequently.
    (B) Occasionally.
    (C) Seldom.
    (D) Never.

50. (A) As a highly developed language.
    (B) As more sophisticated than spoken language.
    (C) As a basic means of communication.
    (D) As an impossible way to communicate.

THIS IS THE END OF THE LISTENING COMPREHENSION SECTION OF THE TEST

THE NEXT PART OF THE TEST IS SECTION 2. TURN TO THE
DIRECTIONS FOR SECTION 2 IN YOUR TEST BOOK.
READ THEM, AND BEGIN WORK.
DO NOT READ OR WORK ON ANY OTHER SECTION OF THE TEST.

  STOP STOP STOP STOP STOP STOP STOP

SECTION 2
STRUCTURE AND WRITTEN EXPRESSION
Time—25 minutes

This section is designed to measure your ability to recognize language that is appropriate for standard written English. There are two types of questions in this section, with special directions for each type.

Directions: Questions 1–15 are incomplete sentences. Beneath each sentence you will see four words or phrases, marked (A), (B), (C), and (D). Choose the one word or phrase that best completes the sentence. Then, on your answer sheet, find the number of the question and fill in the space that corresponds to the letter of the answer you have chosen. Fill in the space so that the letter inside the oval cannot be seen.

Example I

The president _____ the election by a landslide.

(A) won
(B) he won
(C) yesterday
(D) fortunately

Sample Answer

● Ⓑ Ⓒ Ⓓ

The sentence should read, "The president won the election by a landslide." Therefore, you should choose answer (A).

Example II

When _____ the conference?

(A) the doctor attended
(B) did the doctor attend
(C) the doctor will attend
(D) the doctor's attendance

Sample Answer

Ⓐ ● Ⓒ Ⓓ

The sentence should read, "When did the doctor attend the conference?" Therefore, you should choose answer (B).

After you read the directions, begin work on the questions.

1. The adder is a venomous snake _____ bite may prove fatal to humans.

   (A) its
   (B) whom its
   (C) that
   (D) whose

2. The sport of hang gliding _____ by the Federal Aviation Administration (FAA).

   (A) regulated it
   (B) is regulated
   (C) that was regulated
   (D) that it was regulated

PRACTICE TEST ONE

GO ON TO THE NEXT PAGE

3. The javelin used in competition must be between 260 and 270 centimeters _____.

   (A) in length
   (B) it is long
   (C) whose length
   (D) lengthily

4. In an internal combustion engine, _____ and air are heated inside a cylinder.

   (A) and gasoline vapor
   (B) both gasoline vapor
   (C) gasoline vapor additional
   (D) besides gasoline vapor

5. In November of 1863, the city of Atlanta _____ during Sherman's famous "March to the Sea."

   (A) was completely burned
   (B) completely was burned
   (C) it was burned completely
   (D) completely burned it

6. The Kentucky Derby _____ every May at Churchill Downs in Louisville, Kentucky.

   (A) to be run
   (B) run
   (C) it may be run
   (D) is run

7. _____ have captured the spirit of the conquest of America as well as James Fenimore Cooper.

   (A) Few writers
   (B) The few writers
   (C) The writers are few
   (D) Few are the writers

8. Prospectors rushed to Nevada in 1859 _____ was discovered there.

   (A) after gold soon
   (B) soon after gold
   (C) gold was soon after
   (D) they found gold

9. _____ heat from the sun is trapped near the earth's surface, the greenhouse effect occurs.

   (A) Not
   (B) When
   (C) That
   (D) What

10. _____, the outer layer of the skin, contains pigments, pores, and ducts.

    (A) That the epidermis
    (B) The epidermis is
    (C) The epidermis
    (D) The epidermis which

11. The Kilauea volcano _____ on the eastern slope of the larger Mauna Loa volcano.

    (A) is situated
    (B) has situated
    (C) situating
    (D) to situate

12. Out of John Kenneth Galbraith's *The Affluent Society* _____ for an increase in public goods, potentially at the expense of private goods.

    (A) came the argument
    (B) his argument
    (C) argued
    (D) the economist is arguing

13. Unlike the earth, which rotates once every twenty-four hours, _____ once every ten hours.

    (A) the rotation of Jupiter
    (B) the occurrence of Jupiter's rotation
    (C) Jupiter rotates
    (D) Jupiter's rotating

GO ON TO THE NEXT PAGE ➤

14. _____ peaches are classified as freestone or clingstone depends on how difficult it is to remove the pit.

    (A) The
    (B) About
    (C) Whether
    (D) Scientifically

15. Keynes argued that to avoid an economic depression the government _____ spending and lower interest rates.

    (A) is
    (B) higher
    (C) increase
    (D) should increase

Directions: In questions 16–40 each sentence has four underlined words or phrases. The four underlined parts of the sentence are marked (A), (B), (C), and (D). Identify the one underlined word or phrase that must be changed in order for the sentence to be correct. Then, on your answer sheet, find the number of the question and fill in the space that corresponds to the letter of the answer you have chosen.

Example I

The four string on a violin are tuned in fifths.
  A   B   C   D

Sample Answer

Ⓐ ● Ⓒ Ⓓ

The sentence should read, "The four strings on a violin are tuned in fifths." Therefore, you should choose answer (B).

Example II

The research for the book *Roots* taking Alex Haley
    A   B   C
twelve years.
   D

Sample Answer

Ⓐ Ⓑ ● Ⓓ

The sentence should read, "The research for the book *Roots* took Alex Haley twelve years." Therefore, you should choose answer (C).

After you read the directions, begin work on the questions.

16. Soon after the United States' entrance into the war, the major hotels in Atlantic
      A   B   C
City was transformed into military barracks.
     D

17. Major advertising companies have traditionally volunteered its time to public
         A   B   C   D
service accounts.

GO ON TO THE NEXT PAGE

18. The value of <u>precious</u> <u>gems</u> <u>is</u> determined by <u>their</u> hardness, color, and <u>brilliant</u>.
             A   B   C   D

19. <u>Find</u> in 1933, *The New York Sun* <u>was</u> <u>the first</u> successful penny <u>newspaper</u>.
   A   B   C   D

20. The 3,500-foot George Washington Bridge <u>spans</u> <u>the</u> Hudson River <u>to link</u> New York
                                    A   B   C

    City <u>also</u> New Jersey.
          D

21. <u>Some researchers</u> believe that <u>an unfair</u> attitude toward the <u>poor</u> will <u>contributed</u>
              A   B   C   D

    to the problem of poverty.

22. <u>Twenty the</u> amino acids <u>serve</u> <u>as</u> building <u>blocks</u> of proteins.
            A   B C   D

23. Astronomers do not know <u>how many</u> galaxies <u>there are</u>, but <u>is it</u> thought that there
                             A   B   C

    are <u>millions or perhaps billions</u>.
                  D

24. The church <u>it</u> was <u>open</u>, and the choir <u>was having</u> a <u>last minute</u> rehearsal.
               A   B   C   D

25. <u>The most</u> popular <u>breed</u> of dog <u>in the</u> United States are cocker spaniel, poodle, <u>and</u>
      A   B   C   D

    retriever.

26. A <u>water</u> molecule <u>consists of</u> two hydrogen <u>atoms</u> and <u>had</u> one oxygen atom.
      A   B   C   D

27. <u>Once</u> the scientist had figured out the precise path of the comet, he <u>is finding</u> that
    A   B

    he was able <u>to predict</u> <u>its</u> next appearance.
                 C   D

28. The <u>intent of</u> the Historical Society <u>is</u> to restore old buildings and <u>the increase of</u>
         A   B   C

    interest in the history of the <u>area</u>.
                              D

29. The <u>amount</u> of copper sulfate used in the experiment <u>depends</u> <u>from</u> the intensity of
        A   B   C

    the heat.
       D

30. After the yolk is <u>separated</u> <u>from</u> the white, it must be <u>boil</u> <u>immediately</u>.
                  A   B   C   D

GO ON TO THE NEXT PAGE

1. A   16. B
2. B   17. C
3. D   18. B
4. D   19. A
5. B   20. C
6. B   21. C
7. D
8. A
9. B
10. C
11. C
12. D
13. C
14. D
15. A

NORM FASTENERS CO.
CİVATA SANAYİ ve TİC.AŞ.

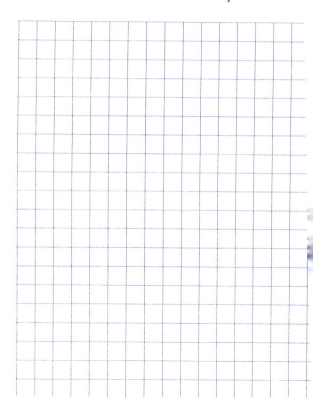

31. At the awards banquet, the philanthropist <u>was recognized</u> for <u>his</u> generosity and
                                              A   B
    <u>careful</u> in <u>aiding</u> the poor.
      C   D

32. <u>Above</u> 80 percent of the <u>laborers</u> at the construction <u>site</u> are <u>temporary</u> workers.
      A   B   C   D

33. The <u>contractings</u> of the <u>heart</u> <u>cause</u> the blood <u>to circulate</u>.
              A   B   C   D

34. The *USS Bonhomme Richard* <u>was</u> commanded by John Paul Jones, <u>that</u> won
                                A   B
    <u>a notable</u> sea battle <u>during</u> the Revolution.
         C   D

35. There <u>exists</u> <u>more than</u> 2,600 different varieties of palm trees, <u>with</u> <u>varying</u> flowers,
            A   B   C   D
    leaves, and fruits.

36. <u>Almost</u> American Indian cultures <u>have been</u> <u>agricultural</u> societies <u>since</u> 2000 B.C.
       A   B   C   D

37. A <u>huge</u> winter storm <u>has</u> brought <u>the</u> snow to Northern California's mountain
        A   B   C
    <u>counties</u>.
       D

38. Nutritionists <u>recommend</u> that foods <u>from each of</u> the four basic groups be <u>eaten</u> on
                    A   B   C
    a <u>regularly</u> daily basis.
        D

39. Neon <u>is often</u> used in airplane beacons because neon beacons are <u>very</u> visible that
           A   B
    <u>they</u> can be <u>seen even</u> through dense fog.
      C   D

40. <u>Her</u> <u>best</u> known <u>role</u> of Judy Garland was <u>as</u> Dorothy in *The Wizard of Oz.*
     A   B   C   D

THIS IS THE END OF SECTION 2

IF YOU FINISH BEFORE TIME IS CALLED, CHECK YOUR WORK
ON SECTION 2 ONLY.
DO NOT READ OR WORK ON ANY OTHER SECTION OF THE TEST.
THE SUPERVISOR WILL TELL YOU WHEN TO BEGIN
WORK ON SECTION 3.

SECTION 3
VOCABULARY AND READING COMPREHENSION
Time—45 minutes

This section is designed to measure your comprehension of standard written English. There are two types of questions in this section, with special directions for each type.

Directions: In questions 1–30 each sentence has an underlined word or phrase. Below each sentence are four other words or phrases, marked (A), (B), (C), and (D). You are to choose the one word or phrase that best keeps the meaning of the original sentence if it is substituted for the underlined word or phrase. Then, on your answer sheet, find the number of the question and fill in the space that corresponds to the letter you have chosen. Fill in the space so that the letter inside the oval cannot be seen.

Example   Sample Answer

Both <u>boats</u> and trains are used for
transporting the materials.

(A) planes
(B) ships
(C) canoes
(D) railroads

The best answer is (B) because "Both ships and trains are used for transporting the materials" is closest in meaning to the original sentence. Therefore, you should choose answer (B).

After you read the directions, begin work on the questions.

1. The new accounts offered by the bank are compounded <u>semi-annually</u>.

   (A) every year
   (B) every six months
   (C) every two years
   (D) every half month

2. The conference is <u>governed</u> by its newly elected board.

   (A) ruled
   (B) chosen
   (C) advised
   (D) watched

3. According to scientists, it is possible that another Ice Age will <u>soon</u> be upon us.

   (A) some day
   (B) now
   (C) in the near future
   (D) undoubtedly

4. Although salamanders are sometimes mistaken for lizards, the two are not <u>related</u>.

   (A) from the same family
   (B) the same size
   (C) of similar appearance
   (D) attached

GO ON TO THE NEXT PAGE

5. The young cancer victim was the most cheerful and most outgoing on the ward.

   (A) frankest
   (B) lightest
   (C) loudest
   (D) happiest

6. Approximately half of American high school graduates enroll in institutions of higher learning.

   (A) buildings
   (B) establishments
   (C) companies
   (D) incidences

7. The members of the committee were assembled quickly.

   (A) advised
   (B) informed
   (C) gathered
   (D) consulted

8. No one knows exactly how many Pacific islands there are, but geographers estimate that there are up to 30,000.

   (A) to the point
   (B) precisely
   (C) approximately
   (D) appropriately

9. A literary award has been established to honor Laura Ingalls Wilder.

   (A) authorize
   (B) please
   (C) vilify
   (D) recognize

10. The largest cactus in the United States is the *saguaro* cactus, found in the areas surrounding the Gulf of California.

    (A) around
    (B) across
    (C) within
    (D) near

11. The solution should be applied, left on for thirty minutes, and rinsed thoroughly.

    (A) completely
    (B) periodically
    (C) roughly
    (D) safely

12. Because of the gravitational pull of the sun, the earth and the other planets maintain an orbit around the sun.

    (A) source
    (B) force
    (C) push
    (D) attractiveness

13. The meat must be chopped before it can be used in that recipe.

    (A) stewed
    (B) bought
    (C) cut
    (D) cooked

14. The wagonmaster decided to ford the stream.

    (A) valley
    (B) mountain
    (C) small river
    (D) plain

15. The first recognized Olympic Games were held in 776 B.C.

    (A) celebrated
    (B) viewed
    (C) acknowledged
    (D) cheered

16. In an annulment, a marriage is declared invalid.

    (A) ill
    (B) unhappy
    (C) unfinished
    (D) void

GO ON TO THE NEXT PAGE

17. The barometer is used by weather forecasters to <u>detect</u> changes in air pressure.

    (A) determine
    (B) mystify
    (C) announce
    (D) reduce

18. From Pavlov's work on conditioned responses in dogs came the stimulus-response theory of <u>behavior</u>.

    (A) thought
    (B) philosophy
    (C) feelings
    (D) conduct

19. Scientists measure the <u>microscopic</u> distances between atoms in microns.

    (A) visible
    (B) tiny
    (C) machine-like
    (D) unmeasured

20. Written divorce <u>regulations</u> first appeared in the <u>legal code</u> of ancient Babylonia.

    (A) rules
    (B) outlines
    (C) regularities
    (D) specifics

21. The Lewis and Clark expedition left St. Louis in 1804 and traveled 7,700 miles <u>enroute to</u> the Pacific Coast.

    (A) away from
    (B) returning to
    (C) on the way to
    (D) leaving

22. Halley's Comet traveled past the Pleiades, a star <u>cluster</u> also known as the Seven Sisters.

    (A) sign
    (B) entity
    (C) projectile
    (D) group

23. When heated to temperatures above 1250 degrees Centigrade, clay <u>fuses</u> and becomes pottery or stoneware.

    (A) burns off
    (B) steams up
    (C) melts together
    (D) decays

24. The three main kinds of tea differ in the <u>method</u> used to process the leaves.

    (A) instructions
    (B) procedure
    (C) development
    (D) variety

25. The speed of light is considered by scientists to be a <u>fundamental</u> constant.

    (A) basic
    (B) contradictory
    (C) necessary
    (D) well-known

26. His hat was knocked <u>askew</u> by the wind.

    (A) awry
    (B) out of shape
    (C) off
    (D) on the ground

27. Although a cheetah can <u>achieve</u> a speed of 110 kilometers <u>per hour</u>, it can maintain this speed for only a few hundred meters.

    (A) race at
    (B) bypass
    (C) uphold
    (D) attain

GO ON TO THE NEXT PAGE

28. A chameleon is a kind of lizard known for its ability to change <u>color</u>.

    (A) scope
    (B) magnitude
    (C) span
    (D) hue

29. The ostrich egg is the largest egg of any <u>nonextinct</u> bird, while the smallest egg is the egg of the hummingbird.

    (A) living
    (B) dead
    (C) flying
    (D) vanished

30. Henry Ford is known for mass producing the Model T, thus making it <u>available to</u> the average American.

    (A) known to
    (B) desired by
    (C) obtainable by
    (D) constructed for

GO ON TO THE NEXT PAGE

Directions: In the rest of this section you will read several passages. Each one is followed by several questions about it. For questions 31–60, you are to choose the one best answer, (A), (B), (C), or (D), to each question. Then, on your answer sheet, find the number of the question and fill in the space that corresponds to the letter of the answer you have chosen.

Answer all questions following a passage on the basis of what is stated or implied in that passage.

Read the following passage:

> John Quincy Adams, who served as the sixth president of the United States from 1825 to 1829, is today recognized for his masterful statesmanship and diplomacy. He dedicated his life to public service, both in the presidency and in the various other political offices he held. Throughout his political career he demonstrated his unswerving belief in freedom of speech, the anti-slavery cause, and the right of Americans to be free from European and Asian domination.

Example I

To what did John Quincy Adams devote his life?

Sample Answer

(A) Improving his personal life
(B) Serving the public
(C) Increasing his fortune
(D) Working on his private business

According to the passage, John Quincy Adams "dedicated his life to public service." Therefore, you should choose answer (B).

Example II

The passage implies that John Quincy Adams held

Sample Answer

(A) no political offices
(B) only one political office
(C) exactly two political offices
(D) at least three political offices

The passage states that John Quincy Adams served in "the presidency and various other political offices." Therefore, you should choose answer (D).

After you read the directions, begin work on the questions.

GO ON TO THE NEXT PAGE ▶

Questions 31–35

The White House, the official home of the United States President, was not built in time for George Washington to live in it. It was begun in 1792 and was ready for its first inhabitants, President and Mrs. John Adams, in 1800. When the Adamses moved in, the White House was not yet complete, and the Adamses suffered many inconveniences. Thomas Jefferson, the third president, improved the comfort of the White House in many respects and added new architectural features such as the terraces on the east and west ends. When British forces burned the White House on August 24, 1814, President Madison was forced to leave, and it was not until 1817 that then President James Monroe was able to return to a rebuilt residence. Since then, the White House has been occupied by each U.S. President.

31. Which of the following would be an appropriate title for this passage?

   (A) George Washington's Life in the White House
   (B) The Burning of the White House
   (C) The Early History of the White House
   (D) Presidential Policies of Early U.S. Presidents

32. Why did George Washington NOT live in the White House?

   (A) It had been burned by the British.
   (B) He did not like the architectural features.
   (C) He did not want to suffer the inconvenience that the Adamses had suffered.
   (D) Construction had not yet been completed.

33. It can be inferred from the passage that John Adams was

   (A) the first president of the United States
   (B) the second president of the United States
   (C) the third president of the United States
   (D) the fourth president of the United States

34. According to the passage, which of the following best describes Thomas Jefferson's tenure in the White House?

   (A) He had to flee the White House because of the war with the British.
   (B) He was accepting of the many inconveniences.
   (C) He removed the terraces that had been added by Adams.
   (D) He worked to improve the appearance and convenience of the White House.

35. According to the passage, when James Monroe came back to the White House, it had been

   (A) repressed
   (B) reconstructed
   (C) relocated
   (D) reserved

GO ON TO THE NEXT PAGE

Questions 36–43

Algae is a primitive form of life, a single-celled or simple multiple-celled organism that is able to conduct the process of photosynthesis. It is generally found in water but can also be found elsewhere, growing on such surfaces as rocks or trees. The various types of algae are classified according to pigment.

Blue-green algae, or *Cyanophyta*, can grow at very high temperatures and under high-intensity light. This type of algae is the oldest form of life with photosynthetic capabilities. Fossilized remains of blue-green algae more than 3.4 billion years old have been found in parts of Africa.

Green algae, or *Chlorophyta*, is generally found in fresh water. It reproduces on the surfaces of enclosed bodies of water such as ponds or lakes and has the appearance of a fuzzy green coating on the surface of the water.

Brown algae, or *Phaeophyta*, grows in shallow, temperate water. This type of algae is the largest in size and is most recognizable as a type of seaweed. Its long stalks can be enmeshed on the ocean floor, or it can float freely on the ocean's surface.

Red algae, or *Rhodophyta*, is a small, delicate organism found in the deep waters of the subtropics. This type of algae has an essential role in the formation of coral reefs: it secretes lime from the seawater to foster the formation of limestone deposits.

36. What is the author's main purpose?

(A) To show what color algae is
(B) To differentiate the various classifications of algae
(C) To describe where algae is found
(D) To clarify the appearance of different types of algae

37. Which of the following is NOT true about algae?

(A) All types have one cell only.
(B) It can be found out of water.
(C) It can use photosynthesis.
(D) It is not a relatively new form of life.

38. The word "pigment" at the end of the first paragraph means

(A) size
(B) shape
(C) composition
(D) color

39. Algae remnants found in Africa are

(A) still flourishing
(B) photogenic
(C) extremely old
(D) red in color

40. Green algae is generally found

(A) on the ocean floor
(B) on top of the water
(C) throughout ponds and lakes
(D) surrounding enclosed bodies of water

41. Brown algae would most likely be found

(A) on trees
(B) near green algae
(C) on rocks
(D) in the ocean

42. According to the passage, red algae is

(A) sturdy
(B) huge
(C) fragile
(D) found in shallow water

43. It can be inferred from the passage that limestone deposits serve as the basis of

(A) coral reefs
(B) red algae
(C) subtropical seawater
(D) secret passages

GO ON TO THE NEXT PAGE

Questions 44–49

Herman Melville, an American author best known today for his novel *Moby Dick*, was actually more popular during his lifetime for some of his other works. He traveled extensively and used the knowledge gained during his travels as the basis for his early novels. In 1837, at the age of eighteen, Melville signed as a cabin boy on a merchant ship that was to sail from his Massachusetts home to Liverpool, England. His experiences on this trip served as a basis for the novel *Redburn* (1849). In 1841 Melville set out on a whaling ship headed for the South Seas. After jumping ship in Tahiti, he wandered around the islands of Tahiti and Moorea. This South Sea island sojourn was a backdrop to the novel *Omoo* (1847). After three years away from home, Melville joined up with a U.S. naval frigate that was returning to the eastern United States around Cape Horn. The novel *White-Jacket* (1850) describes this lengthy voyage as a navy seaman.

With the publication of these early adventure novels, Melville developed a strong and loyal following among readers eager for his tales of exotic places and situations. However, in 1851, with the publication of *Moby Dick*, Melville's popularity started to diminish. *Moby Dick*, on one level the saga of the hunt for the great white whale, was also a heavily symbolic allegory of the heroic struggle of man against the universe. The public was not ready for Melville's literary metamorphosis from romantic adventure to philosophical symbolism. It is ironic that the novel that served to diminish Melville's popularity during his lifetime is the one for which he is best known today.

44. The main subject of the passage is

(A) Melville's travels
(B) the popularity of Melville's novels
(C) Melville's personal background
(D) *Moby Dick*

45. According to the passage, Melville's early novels were

(A) published while he was traveling
(B) completely fictional
(C) all about his work on whaling ships
(D) based on his travels

46. In what year did Melville's book about his experience as a cabin boy appear?

(A) 1837
(B) 1841
(C) 1847
(D) 1849

47. The passage implies that Melville stayed in Tahiti because

(A) he had unofficially left his ship
(B) he was on leave while his ship was in port
(C) he had finished his term of duty
(D) he had received permission to take a vacation in Tahiti

48. How did the publication of *Moby Dick* affect Melville's popularity?

(A) His popularity increased immediately.
(B) It had no effect on his popularity.
(C) It caused his popularity to decrease.
(D) His popularity remained as strong as ever.

49. According to the passage, *Moby Dick*

(A) is a romantic adventure
(B) is a single-faceted work
(C) is a short story about a whale
(D) is symbolic of man fighting his environment

PRACTICE TEST ONE

GO ON TO THE NEXT PAGE

Questions 50–56

Medical bills in the United States have risen outrageously since the beginning of the 1960's, and steps need to be taken to reverse this trend or the average American will not be able to afford medical care. The major factor in increasing the cost of medical care has been the dramatic increase in the cost of hospital services. The rise in the cost of hospitalization can be only partly blamed on inflation since hospital bills in the last two decades have risen at a considerably higher rate than inflation.

Another factor cited by doctors as a major cause for the increase in the cost of medical care is malpractice. Increasingly large awards for malpractice have caused doctors to increase their rates to cover the higher malpractice insurance premiums. Because of the large malpractice awards, doctors are also prescribing more conservative and more extensive—and therefore more costly—treatment for patients as a defense against malpractice claims. Whatever the causes of the wild increases in the cost of medical care, the government needs to take strong action before it is too late for Americans.

50. What is the subject of this passage?

(A) The increasing costs of malpractice insurance
(B) Factors causing the increase in U.S. medical bills
(C) Steps for Americans to take to obtain medical care
(D) The outrageous medical profession

51. According to the passage, how does the author of this passage feel about the tremendous increase in medical bills?

(A) Disquieted
(B) Enthusiastic
(C) Impassive
(D) Apathetic

52. How does the author seem to feel about the tremendous increase in medical bills?

(A) Malpractice insurance
(B) The cost of hospital care
(C) More conservative and expensive prescriptions by doctors
(D) Inflation

53. The passage implies that a slowing in inflation would have what kind of effect on medical costs?

(A) Tremendous
(B) Nonexistent
(C) Slight
(D) Maximum

54. Which of the following is NOT stated in the passage concerning malpractice?

(A) The increase in malpractice insurance is due to inflation.
(B) Malpractice insurance premiums are on the increase.
(C) The increase in malpractice payouts has caused an increase in doctors' bills.
(D) High malpractice awards have caused doctors to work more conservatively.

GO ON TO THE NEXT PAGE

55. What is the author's main point in this passage?

    (A) Inflation is having a terrible effect on medical bills.

    (B) Insurance companies are at fault in raising medical bills.

    (C) Action is needed to counteract increases in medical bills.

    (D) Doctors need to work to decrease malpractice.

56. What does the paragraph following this passage most likely contain?

    (A) A discussion of why the average American will soon be unable to afford medical care

    (B) Forecasts of how inflation will influence medical care in the future

    (C) The tremendous increases in malpractice insurance

    (D) The steps the government could take to curb medical costs

GO ON TO THE NEXT PAGE

Questions 57–60

The Works Progress Administration (WPA), formed during the Great Depression as part of Roosevelt's New Deal, was created with the express intent of putting to work as many as possible of the more than 10 million unemployed in the United States. One of the more controversial programs of the WPA was the Federal Arts Project, a program to employ artists full-time at such tasks as painting murals in libraries, theaters, train stations, and airports; teaching various techniques of art; and preparing a comprehensive study of American crafts. Criticism of the program centered on what was perceived as the frivolity of supporting the arts at a time when millions were starving, industry was sagging, farms were barren, and all that could flourish was bankruptcy courts and soup kitchens.

57. This passage mainly discusses

  (A) the Great Depression
  (B) Franklin Delano Roosevelt's New Deal
  (C) the Federal Arts Project
  (D) bankruptcy courts and soup kitchens

58. According to the passage, the stated purpose of the WPA was to

  (A) create new American masterpieces
  (B) raise the standard of American art
  (C) introduce new art techniques to the American public
  (D) decrease unemployment

59. All the following probably helped to make the Federal Arts Project controversial EXCEPT that

  (A) the Federal Arts Project employed many who would otherwise have been out of work
  (B) trains and airports were decorated with murals
  (C) the Federal Arts Project commissioned art works during the Depression
  (D) a tremendous study of American crafts was produced

60. When the author states that " . . . all that could flourish was bankruptcy courts and soup kitchens," he probably means that

  (A) banks and restaurants did well during the Depression
  (B) the poor could not afford to use banks or eat soup
  (C) the only organizations to thrive were those that dealt with the poor
  (D) many restaurants declared bankruptcy during the Depression

THIS IS THE END OF SECTION 3

IF YOU FINISH BEFORE TIME IS CALLED, CHECK YOUR WORK
ON SECTION 3 ONLY.
DO NOT READ OR WORK ON ANY OTHER SECTION OF THE TEST.

TEST OF WRITTEN ENGLISH: ESSAY QUESTION

Time—30 minutes

Some people argue that vast sums of money should be spent to explore space. Others argue that it is better to solve earth's problems before going out into space. Tell which position you agree with and why.

Write your answer on the answer sheet for the Test of Written English, Practice Test One, on pages 169–170.

PRACTICE TEST TWO

SECTION 1

LISTENING COMPREHENSION

In this section of the test, you will have an opportunity to demonstrate your ability to understand spoken English. There are three parts in this section, with special directions for each part.

Part A

Directions: For each question in Part A, you will hear a short sentence. Each sentence will be spoken just one time. The sentences you hear will not be written out for you. Therefore, you must listen carefully to understand what the speaker says.

After you hear a sentence, read the four choices in your test book, marked (A), (B), (C), and (D), and decide which one is closest in meaning to the sentence you heard. Then, on your answer sheet, find the number of the question and fill in the space that corresponds to the letter of the answer you have chosen. Fill in the space so the letter inside the oval cannot be seen.

Example I   Sample Answer

You will hear: ●
                                                          Ⓑ
You will read: (A) John outran the others.   Ⓒ
                 (B) John was the fastest hunter in   Ⓓ
                     the chase.
                 (C) John wasn't the slowest in the
                     race.
                 (D) John was the last runner to
                     finish the race.

The speaker said, "John was the fastest runner in the race." Sentence (A), "John outran the others," is closest in meaning to the sentence you heard. Therefore, you should choose answer (A).

Example II   Sample Answer

You will hear: Ⓐ
                                                          Ⓑ
You will read: (A) Could you help me use the rest?   ●
                 (B) Do you mind using the other desk?   Ⓓ
                 (C) Would you mind helping me
                     carry this piece of furniture?
                 (D) If you move my desk, I'll help
                     you with your work.

The speaker said, "Could you help me move my desk?" Sentence (C), "Would you mind helping me carry this piece of furniture?" is closest in meaning to the sentence you heard. Therefore, you should choose answer (C).

GO ON TO THE NEXT PAGE ➤

1. (A) I've seen the movie you chose.
   (B) Let's choose something at the movie.
   (C) They decided that I should move.
   (D) I'll accept the movie you recommend.

2. (A) Maria's probably a waitress.
   (B) Maria bought the meal.
   (C) Maria ordered coffee with the meal.
   (D) Coffee was ordered after the meal.

3. (A) The copy's close to the encyclopedia.
   (B) The table has a copy of the magazine on it.
   (C) The encyclopedia table's beside the copy machine.
   (D) The copy machine's on the table.

4. (A) The motor was taken from the train.
   (B) The driver has passed the train.
   (C) The terrorist tried to take over the train.
   (D) The motion of the train was overwhelming.

5. (A) Pat's minding the laundry with Jim.
   (B) Neither Pat nor Jim likes doing the laundry.
   (C) Both Pat and Jim will wash clothes without complaining.
   (D) Pat doesn't mind when Jim does the laundry.

6. (A) She'd rather work alone.
   (B) Group work is her preference.
   (C) She's working on a project about group preferences.
   (D) She projected that the group wouldn't work.

7. (A) I doubt that Bill's portfolio was big.
   (B) Bill has no doubt about his portfolio.
   (C) It's impossible to tell which part of the portfolio's the biggest.
   (D) Bill's portfolio was certainly larger than the others.

8. (A) I don't like the roses.
   (B) I think the roses are lovely.
   (C) Are the roses blooming?
   (D) Are they Betty's roses?

9. (A) Jane usually visits San Francisco for her vacations.
   (B) Jane's cousin often visits San Francisco.
   (C) Whenever there's a holiday, Jane's cousin goes to San Francisco.
   (D) Whenever there's a holiday, Jane leaves San Francisco.

10. (A) The woman moved from the curb into the traffic.
    (B) The nosy woman disturbed the new tenant.
    (C) The woman was bothered by the loud cars and trucks.
    (D) The woman disturbed the traffic with her noise.

11. (A) You went to that restaurant just one time this week.
    (B) Did you go eat there a week ago?
    (C) You just wanted to go to that restaurant to eat.
    (D) Just when the restaurant opened, you went there.

GO ON TO THE NEXT PAGE

PRACTICE TEST TWO

12. (A) Margaret looked in the ditch under the bridge.
    (B) When Margaret looked up, she saw the dictionary.
    (C) Margaret found the meaning of the word.
    (D) Margaret defined what she was looking for.

13. (A) She looks able to finish the exercise.
    (B) It looks like the exercises are complete.
    (C) Her exercises are lacking ability.
    (D) She can't finish her assignment.

14. (A) Mark's working on his schoolwork now.
    (B) Mark's speaking to someone about his math problems.
    (C) Mark must finish his math problems quickly.
    (D) Mark's computed the answers with his calculator.

15. (A) He'll correct the exams this afternoon.
    (B) The exam will be at noon.
    (C) The grader will collect the exams at 12:00.
    (D) The tests will be graded by noon.

16. (A) Mike's name was mentioned to the student council.
    (B) Mike became a member of the student council.
    (C) The council chose Mike as a student.
    (D) Mike was named the best student by the council.

17. (A) The bus trip is only five minutes long.
    (B) You missed the bus by five minutes.
    (C) You should hurry to catch the bus.
    (D) The bus was five minutes late.

18. (A) Bill has prior experience with sick patients.
    (B) Bill has patience with extremely sick people.
    (C) Bill will treat very sick people first.
    (D) Bill will treat any patient with prior exposure to disease.

19. (A) It's a nice, warm spring day.
    (B) For a few weeks this spring, the weather's been warm.
    (C) Although it's spring, it's hot today.
    (D) It's quite a warm day for winter.

20. (A) The amount that he prepared was unbelievable.
    (B) I was surprised that he wasn't ready.
    (C) It was impossible to prepare for his beliefs.
    (D) That he prepared was unbelievable.

Part B

Directions: In Part B you will hear short conversations between two speakers. At the end of each conversation, a third person will ask a question about what was said. You will hear each conversation and question about it just one time. Therefore, you must listen carefully to understand what each speaker says. After you hear a conversation and the question about it, read the four possible answers in your test book and decide

GO ON TO THE NEXT PAGE →

which <u>one</u> is the best answer to the question you heard. Then, on your answer sheet, find the number of the question and fill in the space that corresponds to the letter of the answer you have chosen.

Look at the following example.

You will hear:

You will read: (A) The exam was really awful.
                 (B) It was the worst exam she had ever seen.
                 (C) It couldn't have been more difficult.
                 (D) It wasn't that hard.

Sample Answer

Ⓐ
Ⓑ
Ⓒ
●

From the conversation you learn that the man thought the exam was very difficult and that the woman disagreed with the man. The best answer to the question "What does the woman mean?" is (D), "It wasn't that hard." Therefore, you should choose answer (D).

21. (A) She can't find her briefcase.
    (B) Her briefcase is smaller than his.
    (C) Their briefcases are different sizes.
    (D) He gave his briefcase to her.

22. (A) He found the assignment very difficult.
    (B) The assignment was difficult to complete in thirty minutes.
    (C) The woman couldn't finish the assignment because she had other work to do.
    (D) He finds it hard to believe how much time the woman spent.

23. (A) To drink some coffee in a while.
    (B) To prepare the coffee herself.
    (C) To get the man some coffee later.
    (D) To drink something else.

24. (A) She doesn't want to go to the beach today.
    (B) She doesn't know why the weather's so nice.
    (C) She'd rather be outside today.
    (D) It's not the best time for a walk at the beach.

25. (A) Dinner will get cold.
    (B) The cafeteria will close.
    (C) The line will quickly get too long.
    (D) She'll have dinner somewhere else.

26. (A) Her roommate helped eat some cake.
    (B) She made the cake with some assistance.
    (C) She didn't exactly help her roommate.
    (D) She and her roommate didn't exactly make a cake.

27. (A) The dormitory hours.
    (B) The problem with the rulebook.
    (C) The door number of the dormitory.
    (D) When the dormitory opens.

28. (A) He was just a little upset.
    (B) He was devastated.
    (C) He was a part of the news.
    (D) He felt upset about his hearing.

GO ON TO THE NEXT PAGE

PRACTICE TEST TWO

43

29. (A) He's tired of running.
    (B) He's finished the problem.
    (C) He has to run a race tomorrow.
    (D) He doesn't have enough time.

30. (A) In a restaurant.
    (B) In a grocery store.
    (C) In an airplane.
    (D) At a movie theater.

31. (A) He thought it was fascinating.
    (B) He agreed with the woman.
    (C) He thought it should have been longer.
    (D) He thought it was boring.

32. (A) He wants to get another refrigerator.
    (B) He thinks they need more drinks.
    (C) They have plenty of drinks.
    (D) He doesn't think there are enough.

33. (A) The history paper will get done in time.
    (B) She rarely gets her work done when she should.
    (C) She almost never gets to history class on time.
    (D) She doesn't seem to read the paper before history class.

34. (A) The student decided to park the car.
    (B) The decision was postponed.
    (C) The student council voted on the parking issue.
    (D) The council put the issue on the agenda last week.

35. (A) She only has to attend one meeting.
    (B) She's already attended the meeting.
    (C) She doesn't want to go.
    (D) She'll only attend if she doesn't have plans.

Part C

Directions: In this part of the test, you will hear short talks and conversations. After each of them, you will be asked some questions. You will hear the talks and conversations and the questions about them just one time. They will not be written out for you. Therefore, you must listen carefully to understand what each speaker says.

After you hear a question, read the four possible answers in your test book and decide which one is the best answer to the question you heard. Then, on your answer sheet, find the number of the question and fill in the space that corresponds to the letter of the answer you have chosen.

Listen to this sample talk.

You will hear:

Now look at the following example.

GO ON TO THE NEXT PAGE ➤

You will hear:

You will read: (A) Art from America's inner cities.
(B) Art from the central region of the U.S.
(C) Art from various urban areas in the U.S.
(D) Art from rural sections of America.

Sample Answer

Ⓐ
Ⓑ
Ⓒ
●

The best answer to the question "What style of painting is known as American regionalist?" is (D), "Art from rural sections of America." Therefore, you should choose answer (D).

Now look at the next example.

You will hear:

You will read: (A) *American Regionalist.*
(B) *The Family Farm in Iowa.*
(C) *American Gothic.*
(D) *A Serious Couple.*

Sample Answer

Ⓐ
Ⓑ
●
Ⓓ

The best answer to the question "What is the name of Wood's most successful painting?" is (C), "*American Gothic.*" Therefore, you should choose answer (C).

36. (A) In a bookstore.
(B) At a history lecture.
(C) On a university campus.
(D) In the advertising department of a newspaper.

37. (A) The price of textbooks.
(B) History 101.
(C) The university bookstore.
(D) Ways to sell a used book.

38. (A) He desperately needs the money.
(B) Reading doesn't interest him.
(C) He's finished using them.
(D) He'd rather have cheaper books.

39. (A) The bookstore doesn't want to buy them.
(B) He wouldn't get enough money.
(C) He doesn't like the bookstore's advertisements.
(D) It's too late to sell them to the bookstore.

40. (A) He should post some advertisements.
(B) He should take History 101.
(C) He should give the books to the bookstore for nothing.
(D) He should keep the books.

41. (A) The Central Pacific group.
(B) The Transcontinental Railroad Company.
(C) A group from Ogden, Utah.
(D) Two separate railroad companies.

GO ON TO THE NEXT PAGE

42. (A) They had to lay tracks across a mountain range.
    (B) They had to cross all of Nebraska.
    (C) They had to work for another railroad company.
    (D) They had to move westward to Sacramento, California.

43. (A) Ceremonious.
    (B) Exhilarating.
    (C) Dangerous.
    (D) Exuberant.

44. (A) Several days.
    (B) Several weeks.
    (C) Several months.
    (D) Several years.

45. (A) Dynamite was used to blast out access.
    (B) A golden spike was used to complete the tracks.
    (C) The workers labored dangerously and exhaustingly.
    (D) The workers traversed the Sierra Nevadas.

46. (A) From a friend.
    (B) From the newspaper.
    (C) From a discussion.
    (D) From the utility company.

47. (A) In a far desert.
    (B) Close by.
    (C) At the utility company's headquarters.
    (D) The man has no idea.

48. (A) It's cheaper in the short run.
    (B) The utility company won't need any extra money.
    (C) The plant's far away.
    (D) It exists in large quantities.

49. (A) The cost is extremely low.
    (B) The costs outweigh the benefits.
    (C) It'll be worth it in the long term.
    (D) Money's abundant to finance the plant.

50. (A) She's concerned it'll be too costly.
    (B) She thinks the price is too low.
    (C) She thinks the plant is totally unnecessary.
    (D) She thinks the utility company has a good idea.

THIS IS THE END OF THE LISTENING COMPREHENSION SECTION OF THE TEST

THE NEXT PART OF THE TEST IS SECTION 2. TURN TO THE DIRECTIONS FOR SECTION 2 IN YOUR TEST BOOK.
READ THEM, AND BEGIN WORK.
DO NOT READ OR WORK ON ANY OTHER SECTION OF THE TEST.

STOP STOP STOP STOP STOP STOP STOP

SECTION 2
STRUCTURE AND WRITTEN EXPRESSION
Time—25 minutes

This section is designed to measure your ability to recognize language that is appropriate for standard written English. There are two types of questions in this section, with special directions for each type.

<u>Directions:</u>   Questions 1–15 are incomplete sentences. Beneath each sentence you will see four words or phrases, marked (A), (B), (C), and (D). Choose the <u>one</u> word or phrase that best completes the sentence. Then, on your answer sheet, find the number of the question and fill in the space that corresponds to the letter of the answer you have chosen. Fill in the space so that the letter inside the oval cannot be seen.

Example I   Sample Answer

The president _____ the election
by a landslide.

(A) won
(B) he won
(C) yesterday
(D) fortunately

The sentence should read, "The president won the election by a landslide." Therefore, you should choose answer (A).

Example II   Sample Answer

When _____ the conference?

(A) the doctor attended
(B) did the doctor attend
(C) the doctor will attend
(D) the doctor's attendance

The sentence should read, "When did the doctor attend the conference?" Therefore, you should choose answer (B).

After you read the directions, begin work on the questions.

1. The human body has four jugular
    veins, _____ each side of the neck.

    (A) there are two on
    (B) it has two on
    (C) two are on
    (D) two on

2. In 1905 Juneau replaced Sitka
    _____ Alaska.

    (A) the capital was
    (B) as the capital of
    (C) was the capital of
    (D) the capital being

PRACTICE TEST TWO   GO ON TO THE NEXT PAGE ➤

3. _____ of the Stamp Act in 1865 provoked strong opposition among the American colonists.

   (A) The passage was
   (B) It was the passage
   (C) Before the passage
   (D) The passage

4. _____ were first viewed through a telescope by Galileo.

   (A) Jupiter has four moons
   (B) Jupiter's four moons
   (C) Jupiter surrounded by four moons
   (D) Surrounded by four moons, Jupiter

5. _____ the end of the Ice Age around 8000 B.C., mammoths became extinct.

   (A) With
   (B) It was
   (C) That
   (D) In addition

6. The gila monster is _____ poisonous lizards found in North America.

   (A) few
   (B) the one
   (C) one of the few
   (D) of the one few

7. _____ New Jersey's proximity to New York, it is an important link in the nation's transportation system.

   (A) Since
   (B) Resulting
   (C) However
   (D) Because of

8. Agronomists work to improve the quality of crops, increase the yield of fields, and _____ of the soil.

   (A) the quality is maintained
   (B) maintain the quality
   (C) the maintenance of the quality
   (D) maintaining the quality

9. From 1898 to 1933, the U.S. Weather Bureau obtained information about the weather from _____ to box kites.

   (A) attached devices
   (B) attached to devices
   (C) devices attached
   (D) devices were attached

10. Projective tests _____ as the Rorschach Test have no right or wrong answers.

    (A) such
    (B) similar
    (C) like
    (D) same

11. One purpose _____ to decide if there is sufficient evidence to try a person for a crime.

    (A) of a grand jury is
    (B) of a grand jury
    (C) for a grand jury
    (D) of a grand jury which is

12. _____ in 1937, the Golden Gate Bridge spans the channel at the entrance to San Francisco Bay.

    (A) Completes
    (B) Completed
    (C) Completing
    (D) To complete

13. A slipped disk is a condition _____ the intervertebral disk protrudes and presses on nerves.

    (A) what
    (B) which is
    (C) in which
    (D) that

GO ON TO THE NEXT PAGE

14. There are two basic kinds of air compressors, reciprocating and _____.

    (A) another kind that is rotating
    (B) one that rotates
    (C) a rotating kind
    (D) rotating

15. When _____ of impulses from many of the neurons in one part of the brain, an epileptic seizure occurs.

    (A) the simultaneous bursts
    (B) simultaneously burst
    (C) there are simultaneous bursts
    (D) simultaneously bursting

Directions: In questions 16–40 each sentence has four underlined words or phrases. The four underlined parts of the sentence are marked (A), (B), (C), and (D). Identify the one underlined word or phrase that must be changed in order for the sentence to be correct. Then, on your answer sheet, find the number of the question and fill in the space that corresponds to the letter of the answer you have chosen.

Example I

The four string on a violin are tuned in fifths.
        A   B   C   D

Sample Answer
Ⓐ
●
Ⓒ
Ⓓ

The sentence should read, "The four strings on a violin are tuned in fifths." Therefore, you should choose answer (B).

Example II

The research for the book *Roots* taking Alex Haley
    A   B   C
twelve years.
    D

Sample Answer
Ⓐ
Ⓑ
●
Ⓓ

The sentence should read, "The research for the book *Roots* took Alex Haley twelve years." Therefore, you should choose answer (C).

After you read the directions, begin work on the questions.

16. Latex rubber is made from a milky substantial in plants and trees of the sapodilla
                     A   B   C   D
    family.

17. The state with the most large production of tobacco products is North Carolina.
             A   B   C   D

18. Alfalfa is a nutritious crop rich in proteins, minerals, and with vitamins.
         A   B   C   D

19. <u>The first</u> professional baseball game <u>it</u> took place in 1846 <u>when the</u> New York Nine
      A   B   C

    <u>defeated</u> the New York Knickerbockers 23 to 1.
      D

20. <u>More than</u> 300 different <u>kinds</u> of nails <u>is</u> <u>manufactured</u> in the United States.
        A   B   C   D

21. <u>Among</u> Thomas Jefferson's many <u>accomplishment</u> was <u>his</u> work <u>to establish</u> the
      A   B   C   D

    University of Virginia.

22. The state of New Mexico <u>is not</u> densely <u>population,</u> <u>with an</u> average of <u>only</u> four
                                   A   B   C   D

    people per square kilometer.

23. <u>Alike</u> bases <u>which</u> cause litmus to turn blue, <u>acids</u> <u>cause</u> litmus to turn red.
      A   B   C   D

24. Plant cuttings <u>who</u> are <u>placed</u> in water will develop roots and can <u>then be</u> planted
                   A   B   C

    <u>in soil</u>.
      D

25. Lead <u>poisoning</u> can result if <u>to</u> much lead <u>builds up</u> in <u>the body</u>.
         A   B   C   D

26. Many American <u>childrens</u> learned <u>to read</u> <u>the</u> <u>more than</u> 120 million copies of
               A   B C   D

    McGuffy's Reader.

27. In *A Farewell to Arms* (1926), Hemingway <u>tried</u> <u>to capture</u> the <u>feelings the</u> American
                                            A   B   C

    people at <u>the end of</u> World War I.
              D

28. <u>When mining</u> for gold, you <u>must first</u> obtain the gold ore <u>and then</u> <u>apart</u> the gold from
         A   B   C   D

    the ore.

29. From 1785 to 1790, <u>the</u> <u>capital</u> of the U.S. <u>will be</u> <u>located</u> in New York City.
                       A   B   C   D

30. The water in the Great Salt Lake is <u>at less</u> <u>four times</u> <u>saltier</u> <u>than</u> seawater.
                                       A   B   C   D

GO ON TO THE NEXT PAGE

31. When T. S. Eliot's *The Wasteland* appeared in 1922, <u>critics</u> were divided <u>as to</u> how

A   B
    <u>good</u> it was <u>written</u>.

C   D

32. The Wagner Act <u>guarantees</u> <u>workers</u> in the U.S. <u>the right</u> to <u>organizing</u> labor unions.

          A   B   C   D

33. Ships are able <u>to move through</u> canals <u>because locks</u>, <u>rectangular</u> areas with <u>varying</u>

              A   B   C   D
    water levels.

34. The <u>average</u> salt <u>content</u> of seawater is <u>more than</u> three <u>percents</u>.

     A   B   C   D

35. John Hancock <u>was</u> <u>the first</u> to <u>do</u> <u>his signature</u> on the Declaration of Independence.

           A   B   C   D

36. It is in the troposphere, <u>the lowest part</u> of the atmosphere, that wind, <u>stormy</u>, and

                        A   B
    <u>other kinds</u> of weather <u>take place</u>.

   C   D

37. The <u>isotopes</u> of <u>one element</u> can have <u>different</u> <u>weighs</u>.

    A   B   C   D

38. <u>Of</u> <u>the two</u> Diomede Islands, <u>only</u> one <u>belongs the</u> United States.

A B   C   D

39. The novels of Kurt Vonnegut <u>present</u> a <u>desperately</u> comic <u>aware</u> of <u>human nature</u>.

                      A   B   C   D

40. <u>In spite of</u> her <u>physician</u> handicaps, Helen Keller <u>graduated</u> <u>from</u> Radcliffe with

   A   B   C   D
    honors.

THIS IS THE END OF SECTION 2

IF YOU FINISH BEFORE TIME IS CALLED, CHECK YOUR WORK
ON SECTION 2 ONLY.
DO NOT READ OR WORK ON ANY OTHER SECTION OF THE TEST.
THE SUPERVISOR WILL TELL YOU WHEN TO BEGIN
WORK ON SECTION 3.

SECTION 3
VOCABULARY AND READING COMPREHENSION
Time—45 minutes

This section is designed to measure your comprehension of standard written English. There are two types of questions in this section, with special directions for each type.

Directions: In questions 1–30 each sentence has an underlined word or phrase. Below each sentence are four other words or phrases, marked (A), (B), (C), and (D). You are to choose the one word or phrase that best keeps the meaning of the original sentence if it is substituted for the underlined word or phrase. Then, on your answer sheet, find the number of the question and fill in the space that corresponds to the letter you have chosen. Fill in the space so that the letter inside the oval cannot be seen.

Example   Sample Answer

    Both boats and trains are used for   Ⓐ
    transporting the materials.   ●
                                                                 Ⓒ
    (A)   planes   Ⓓ
    (B)   ships
    (C)   canoes
    (D)   railroads

The best answer is (B) because "Both ships and trains are used for transporting the materials" is closest in meaning to the original sentence. Therefore, you should choose answer (B).

After you read the directions, begin work on the questions.

1. The mission at San Juan Capistrano was partially destroyed by an earthquake in 1812.

    (A)   partly
    (B)   briefly
    (C)   intentionally
    (D)   purposefully

2. Quality control is an essential aspect of the manufacturing process.

    (A)   an alternative
    (B)   an introspective
    (C)   an encompassing
    (D)   a necessary

3. Almost one half of the world's almonds are produced in California.

    (A)   Barely
    (B)   Entirely
    (C)   Nearly
    (D)   Scarcely

4. Frank Borman was the commander of the Apollo 8 space flight when it circled the moon in 1968.

    (A)   traveled to
    (B)   went around
    (C)   reached
    (D)   spanned

 GO ON TO THE NEXT PAGE

5. When Benjamin Franklin became the first American postmaster general in 1775, he worked to improve the frequency and <u>reliability</u> of mail delivery.

   (A) satisfaction
   (B) opportunity
   (C) dependability
   (D) extent

6. Most magazines are <u>financed</u> with revenues received from advertising, subscription sales, and newsstand sales.

   (A) funded
   (B) matched
   (C) stated
   (D) enriched

7. A human body requires more nutrients in cold weather because more energy is necessary to <u>maintain</u> body temperature.

   (A) surpass
   (B) preserve
   (C) equip
   (D) reach

8. Some economists are proposing that the United States institute a consumption tax <u>rather than</u> an income tax.

   (A) in addition to
   (B) in place of
   (C) at the expense of
   (D) alongside

9. The squid's giant nerve fibers are used by <u>marine</u> biologists to conduct research on how nerves work.

   (A) aquatic
   (B) military
   (C) seafaring
   (D) naval

10. Neutron stars are incredibly dense stars that are formed after the <u>explosion</u> of a supernova.

    (A) brilliance
    (B) dynamism
    (C) expansion
    (D) burst

11. In the Taft-Hartley Act of 1947, the closed shop became <u>illegal</u>.

    (A) uncertain
    (B) open
    (C) prohibited
    (D) lawful

12. In the United States, election campaign spending and <u>contributions</u> are regulated by the government.

    (A) buying
    (B) taxation
    (C) donations
    (D) charities

13. To correct nearsightedness, most patients wear lenses that are <u>thicker</u> at the edges than in the middle.

    (A) heavier
    (B) wider
    (C) duller
    (D) more transparent

14. There are three <u>key</u> elements in Darwin's theory of natural selection.

    (A) crucial
    (B) intangible
    (C) stated
    (D) retractable

15. A nurse practitioner has training in <u>a specialized</u> area of medicine.

    (A) an honorable
    (B) a difficult
    (C) a prescribed
    (D) a distinct

GO ON TO THE NEXT PAGE

16. The White House attracts 30,000 visitors each week.

    (A) lures
    (B) beautifies
    (C) implements
    (D) pleases

17. Crop irrigation has long played a role in agricultural practices.

    (A) possibilities
    (B) routines
    (C) rehearsals
    (D) services

18. Three major United States television networks, ABC, CBS, and NBC, are headquartered in New York City.

    (A) in competition in
    (B) centered in
    (C) moving to
    (D) broadcast from

19. Many desert animals have made adaptations that are strikingly similar to those of desert plants.

    (A) predominantly
    (B) precipitously
    (C) forcefully
    (D) remarkably

20. In the early 1960's many Southern communities were slow to desegregate their public schools.

    (A) establishments
    (B) communes
    (C) states
    (D) neighborhoods

21. Oats were often harvested with a machine called a combine.

    (A) ground
    (B) packaged
    (C) gathered
    (D) planted

22. Scientists believe that a 400-mile wide meteoric crater to the east of Hudson Bay may be the world's largest.

    (A) container
    (B) depression
    (C) locale
    (D) mound

23. Congressional leaders prepared a strategy to override the presidential veto.

    (A) reverse
    (B) transport
    (C) celebrate
    (D) dissipate

24. The macadamia tree, originally an Australian evergreen, was brought to Hawaii in the 1800's, and today its nuts are an important Hawaiian crop.

    (A) houseplant
    (B) natural resource
    (C) endangered species
    (D) farm product

25. The "New Deal" was President Franklin D. Roosevelt's plan to counteract the economic hardship of the Depression.

    (A) repress
    (B) resurrect
    (C) alleviate
    (D) defend

26. Grandma Moses, famous for her simplistic scenes of rural life, began painting at the age of 76.

    (A) country
    (B) suburban
    (C) slow-paced
    (D) primitive

GO ON TO THE NEXT PAGE

27. Practitioners of behavioral medicine <u>encourage</u> patients to be responsible for their own health.

   (A) urge
   (B) enlighten
   (C) allow
   (D) admonish

28. George Washington's armies set up <u>an encampment</u> at Morristown, New Jersey, for two winters during the American Revolution.

   (A) an encounter
   (B) a bivouac
   (C) an encroachment
   (D) a detainment

29. In the 1960's the upper level of Pennsylvania Station in New York City was <u>torn down</u> and replaced by Madison Square Garden.

   (A) detracted
   (B) demoted
   (C) distended
   (D) dismantled

30. After twenty-two <u>straight</u> days of rain, the Illinois governor called out the National Guard to deal with the disaster.

   (A) consecutive
   (B) oppressive
   (C) negligent
   (D) cataclysmic

<u>Directions:</u> In the rest of this section you will read several passages. Each one is followed by several questions about it. For questions 31–60, you are to choose the <u>one</u> best answer, (A), (B), (C), or (D), to each question. Then, on your answer sheet, find <u>the</u> number of the question and fill in the space that corresponds to the letter of the answer you have chosen.

Answer all questions following a passage on the basis of what is <u>stated</u> or <u>implied</u> in that passage.

Read the following passage:

> John Quincy Adams, who served as the sixth president of the United States from 1825 to 1829, is today recognized for his masterful statesmanship and diplomacy. He dedicated his life to public service, both in the presidency and in the various other political offices he held. Throughout his political career he demonstrated his unswerving belief in freedom of speech, the anti-slavery cause, and the right of Americans to be free from European and Asian domination.

Example I

To what did John Quincy Adams devote his life?

   (A) Improving his personal life
   (B) Serving the public
   (C) Increasing his fortune
   (D) Working on his private business

Sample Answer

Ⓐ
●
Ⓒ
Ⓓ

According to the passage, John Quincy Adams "dedicated his life to public service." Therefore, you should choose answer (B).

PRACTICE TEST TWO

 GO ON TO THE NEXT PAGE

Example II   Sample Answer

The passage implies that John
Quincy Adams held
                                                              Ⓐ
                                                              Ⓑ
                                                              Ⓒ
(A) no political offices   ⬤
(B) only one political office
(C) exactly two political offices
(D) at least three political offices

The passage states that John Quincy Adams served in "the presidency and various other political offices." Therefore, you should choose answer (D).

After you read the directions, begin work on the questions.

Questions 31–34

The deer is a distinctive animal easily recognized by the antlers that adorn most species of male deer. These antlers are used by the males primarily to fight, either for mates or for leadership of the herd. Deer generally lose their antlers each winter and begin growing new ones in late spring. The new antlers are soft knobs covered with velvety hairs. Later in the year as the seasons progress, the antlers grow and harden into solid branches. In the middle of winter, the full-grown antlers fall off and decay on the ground. The following spring the process begins again.

31. The deer is called a distinctive animal because it

(A) uses its antlers to recognize others
(B) has many species
(C) has antlers
(D) has to fight for its mates

32. According to the passage, the deer does NOT use its antlers

(A) to battle other deer
(B) to get a mate
(C) to become a leader
(D) to climb branches

33. In which month would a deer probably have short, soft, velvety antlers?

(A) May
(B) December
(C) October
(D) January

34. In winter the mature antlers

(A) are soft knobs
(B) come off
(C) are covered with velvety hair
(D) begin again

GO ON TO THE NEXT PAGE

Questions 35–39

Samuel Morse accomplished something that is rarely accomplished: he achieved fame and success in two widely differing areas. Throughout his youth he studied art, and after graduating from Yale University he went on to London in 1811 where his early artistic endeavors met with acclaim. In London he was awarded the gold medal of the Adelphi Arts Society for a clay figure of Hercules, and his paintings *The Dying Hercules* and *The Judgement of Jupiter* were selected for exhibit by the Royal Academy. Later in life, after returning to America, Morse became known for his portraits. His portraits of the Marquis de Lafayette today are on exhibit in the New York City Hall and the New York Public Library.

In addition to his artistic accomplishments, Morse is also well-known today for his work developing the telegraph and what is known as Morse Code. He first had the idea of trying to develop the telegraph in 1832, on board a ship returning to America from Europe. It took eleven long years of ridicule by his associates, disinterest by the public, and a shortage of funds before Congress finally allocated $30,000 to Morse for his project. With these funds, Morse hung a telegraph line from Washington, D.C. to Baltimore, and on May 24, 1844, a message in the dots and dashes of Morse Code was successfully transmitted.

35. Which of the following is the best topic of this passage?

(A) Samuel Morse's artistic talents
(B) The use of Morse Code in art
(C) The invention of the telegraph
(D) Samuel Morse's varied successes

36. According to the passage, in his early life, Morse concentrated on preparing for which of the following careers?

(A) A career as an inventor
(B) A career as an artist
(C) A career as a telegraph operator
(D) A career developing Morse Code

37. According to the passage, Morse won a prize for which of the following works?

(A) A statue of Hercules
(B) *The Dying Hercules*
(C) *The Judgement of Jupiter*
(D) A portrait of Lafayette

38. According to the passage, which of the following best describes the development of the telegraph?

(A) It was a long and difficult process.
(B) It happened almost overnight.
(C) Morse's friends were highly supportive of his work.
(D) Money was not an issue in the development of the telegraph.

39. How was the first telegraph message sent from Washington to Baltimore?

(A) A voice was transmitted over the wires.
(B) The telegraph line carried a written message.
(C) The message was in a special code developed by Morse.
(D) Funds were transmitted from Washington to Baltimore.

GO ON TO THE NEXT PAGE

Questions 40–44

In the beginning of the nineteenth century, the American educational system was desperately in need of reform. Private schools existed, but only for the very rich, and there were very few public schools because of the strong sentiment that a child who would grow up to be a laborer should not "waste" his time on education but should instead prepare himself for his life's work. It was in the face of this public sentiment that educational reformers set about their task. Horace Mann, probably the most famous of the reformers, felt that there was no excuse in a republic for any citizen to be uneducated. As Superintendent of Education in the state of Massachusetts from 1837 to 1848, he initiated various changes, which were soon matched in other school districts around the country. He extended the school year from five to six months and improved the quality of teachers by instituting teacher education and raising teacher salaries. Although these changes did not bring about a sudden improvement in the educational system, they at least increased public awareness as to the need for a further strengthening of the system.

40. It is implied in the passage that to go to a private school, a student needed

   (A) a high level of intelligence
   (B) a strong educational background
   (C) good grades
   (D) a lot of money

41. Why is the word "waste" (line 4) punctuated in this manner?

   (A) The author wants to emphasize how much time was wasted on education.
   (B) The author is quoting someone else who said that education was a waste of time.
   (C) The author thinks that education is not really a waste of time.
   (D) The author does not want students to waste their time on education.

42. According to the passage, why did Horace Mann want a better educational system for Americans?

   (A) Education at the time was so cheap.
   (B) In a republic, all the citizens should be educated.
   (C) People had nothing else to do except go to school.
   (D) Massachusetts residents needed something to do with their spare time.

43. According to the passage, which of the following is a change that Horace Mann instituted?

   (A) Better teacher training
   (B) Increased pay for students
   (C) The five-month school year
   (D) The matching of other districts' policies

44. Which of the following would be the most appropriate title for the passage?

   (A) A Fight for Change
   (B) Nineteenth-Century Reform
   (C) American Education
   (D) The Beginnings of Reform in American Education

GO ON TO THE NEXT PAGE

Questions 45–49

Biofeedback is on the verge of becoming an important tool in medical therapy. Using biofeedback, a patient can learn to control certain body systems, such as heartbeat, temperature, or blood pressure, that are normally autonomic or self-regulating. The patient is attached to a machine measuring the function he wishes to control. When the desired result is achieved, the patient hears a steady tone that indicates that the patient has successfully manipulated that body function to a more desirable state. For example, if a patient wishes to learn to control his heartbeat, he is attached to a biofeedback machine monitoring his heartbeat. When the patient manages to successfully slow his heart beat, the biofeedback machine rewards him with a low, dull noise. Today researchers are using biofeedback to treat patients with such maladies as irregular heartbeat, migraine headaches, and high blood pressure. The medical community foresees myriad applications that may be treated with biofeedback in the future.

45. The main purpose of this passage is to

    (A) describe a medical technique that is being used extensively today throughout the medical community
    (B) describe a new, potentially helpful medical treatment
    (C) teach patients how to use biofeedback machines
    (D) explain how a patient uses biofeedback to control his heartbeat

46. According to the passage, what is an *autonomic* body process?

    (A) Self-controlling
    (B) Usual
    (C) Consciously regulated
    (D) Disorganized

47. According to the passage, how does a patient know that he has achieved a desired result when using a biofeedback machine?

    (A) The machine records the results.
    (B) He hears a sound.
    (C) The doctor gives him a reward.
    (D) The machine monitors the process.

48. Which of the following medical problems would probably NOT be treated by biofeedback?

    (A) A tension headache
    (B) Fever
    (C) Irregular heart rhythm
    (D) A broken leg

49. According to the passage, what do medical authorities see in the future for biofeedback?

    (A) Numerous problems
    (B) Decreased implementation
    (C) Many different uses
    (D) Rejection by the medical community

GO ON TO THE NEXT PAGE

Questions 50–54

Niagara Falls, one of the most famous North American natural wonders, has long been a popular tourist destination. Tourists today flock to see the two falls that actually comprise Niagara Falls: the 53-meter high Horseshoe Falls on the Canadian side of the Niagara River and the 55-meter high American Falls on the U.S. side of the river. Most visitors come between April and October, and it is quite a popular activity to take a steamer out on to the river and right up to the base of the falls for a close-up view. It is also possible to get a spectacular view of the falls from the strategic locations along the Niagara River such as Prospect Point or Table Rock, or from one of the four observation towers which have heights up to 500 feet.

Tourists have been visiting Niagara Falls in large numbers since the 1800's. Because of concern that the large number of tourists would destroy the natural beauty of this scenic wonder, the State of New York in 1885 created Niagara Falls Park in order to protect the land surrounding American Falls. A year later Canada created Queen Victoria Park on the Canadian side of the Niagara, around Horseshoe Falls.

50. According to the passage, which best describes Niagara Falls?

   (A) Niagara Falls consists of two rivers, one Canadian and the other American.
   (B) American Falls is considerably higher than Horseshoe Falls.
   (C) The Niagara River has two falls, one in Canada and one in the U.S.
   (D) Although the Niagara river flows through the U.S. and Canada, the falls are only in the U.S.

51. The passage implies that tourists prefer

   (A) to visit Niagara Falls during warmer weather
   (B) to see the falls from a great distance
   (C) to take a ride over the falls
   (D) to come to Niagara Falls for a winter vacation

52. What is a "steamer" (middle of the first paragraph)?

   (A) A bus
   (B) A boat
   (C) A walkway
   (D) A park

53. According to the passage, why was Niagara Park created?

   (A) To encourage tourists to visit Niagara Falls
   (B) To show off the natural beauty of Niagara Falls
   (C) To protect the area around Niagara Falls
   (D) To force Canada to open Queen Victoria Park

54. What is the major point the author is making in this passage?

   (A) Niagara Falls can be viewed from either the American side or the Canadian side.
   (B) A trip to the U.S. isn't complete without a visit to Niagara Falls.
   (C) Niagara Falls has had an interesting history.
   (D) It has been necessary to protect Niagara Falls from the many tourists who go there.

GO ON TO THE NEXT PAGE

Questions 55–60

Rock and soil samples brought back from the moon by the Apollo astronauts have taught scientists much about the composition of the moon. Moon soil contains small bits of rock and glass and was probably ground from larger rocks when meteors impacted with the surface of the moon. Scientists found no trace of animal or plant life in the moon soil. In addition to the moon soil, astronauts gathered two basic types of rocks from the surface of the moon: *basalt* and *breccia*. Basalt is a cooled and hardened volcanic lava common to the earth. Since basalt is formed under extremely high temperatures, the presence of this type of rock is an indication that the temperature of the moon was once extremely hot. Breccia, the other kind of rock brought back by the astronauts, was formed during the impact of falling objects on the surface of the moon. This second type of rock consists of small pieces of rock compressed together by the force of impact. Gases such as hydrogen and helium were found in some of the rocks, and scientists believe that these gases were carried to the moon on the streams of gases that are constantly emitted from the sun.

55. Which of the following would be the most appropriate title for this passage?

  (A) The Apollo Astronauts
  (B) Soil on the Moon
  (C) What the Moon is Made of
  (D) Basalt and Breccia

56. According to the passage, what does moon soil consist of?

  (A) Hydrogen and helium
  (B) Large chunks of volcanic lava
  (C) Tiny pieces of stones and glass
  (D) Streams of gases

57. Which of the following was NOT brought back to the earth by the astronauts?

  (A) Basalt
  (B) Soil
  (C) Breccia
  (D) Plant life

58. According to the passage, breccia was formed

  (A) when objects struck the moon
  (B) from volcanic lava
  (C) when streams of gases hit the surface of the moon
  (D) from the interaction of helium and hydrogen

59. According to the passage, what do scientists believe about the gases found in the moon rocks?

  (A) The gases came to the moon from the sun.
  (B) The gases were created inside the rocks.
  (C) The streams of gases went to the sun.
  (D) The emittance of the gases caused the moon's temperature to rise.

GO ON TO THE NEXT PAGE

60. The author's purpose in this passage is to

(A) describe some rock and soil samples
(B) explain some of the things man has learned from space flights
(C) propose a new theory about the creation of the moon
(D) demonstrate the difference between *basalt* and *breccia*

THIS IS THE END OF SECTION 3

IF YOU FINISH BEFORE TIME IS CALLED, CHECK YOUR WORK
ON SECTION 3 ONLY.
DO NOT READ OR WORK ON ANY OTHER SECTION OF THE TEST.

STOP STOP STOP STOP STOP STOP STOP

TEST OF WRITTEN ENGLISH: ESSAY QUESTION

Time—30 minutes

Study the following graph describing characteristics of three candidates for promotion to the position of supervisor. Then respond to the question.

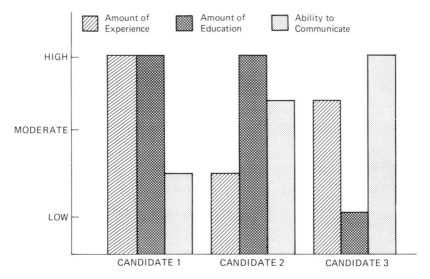

Three Candidates for Promotion

You are to decide which of the three candidates should be promoted to the position of supervisor in your company. Choose one of the three candidates based on the information in the graph. Then explain your choice.

Write your answer on the answer sheet for the Test of Written English, Practice Test Two, on pages 173–174.

SECTION 1
LISTENING COMPREHENSION

In this section of the test, you will have an opportunity to demonstrate your ability to understand spoken English. There are three parts in this section, with special directions for each part.

Part A

Directions: For each question in Part A, you will hear a short sentence. Each sentence will be spoken just one time. The sentences you hear will not be written out for you. Therefore, you must listen carefully to understand what the speaker says.

After you hear a sentence, read the four choices in your test book, marked (A), (B), (C), and (D), and decide which <u>one</u> is closest in meaning to the sentence you heard. Then, on your answer sheet, find the number of the question and fill in the space that corresponds to the letter of the answer you have chosen. Fill in the space so the letter inside the oval cannot be seen.

Example I   Sample Answer

You will hear: ● Ⓑ Ⓒ Ⓓ

You will read: (A) John outran the others.
                 (B) John was the fastest hunter in
                     the chase.
                 (C) John wasn't the slowest in the
                     race.
                 (D) John was the last runner to
                     finish the race.

The speaker said, "John was the fastest runner in the race." Sentence (A), "John outran the others," is closest in meaning to the sentence you heard. Therefore, you should choose answer (A).

Example II   Sample Answer

You will hear: Ⓐ Ⓑ ● Ⓓ

You will read: (A) Could you help me use the rest?
                 (B) Do you mind using the other desk?
                 (C) Would you mind helping me
                     carry this piece of furniture?
                 (D) If you move my desk, I'll help
                     you with your work.

The speaker said, "Could you help me move my desk?" Sentence (C), "Would you mind helping me carry this piece of furniture?" is closest in meaning to the sentence you heard. Therefore, you should choose answer (C).

64   PRACTICE TEST THREE

GO ON TO THE NEXT PAGE ▶

1. (A) Will you take a flight?
    (B) Do you have to fly?
    (C) What time's your departure?
    (D) When will you arrive?

2. (A) The room could've been smaller.
    (B) The room wasn't big enough.
    (C) It was necessary to have such a big room.
    (D) The room wasn't very big.

3. (A) The teacher read one chapter per week.
    (B) The teacher recommended reading one chapter per week.
    (C) The teacher and the students read one chapter on the weekend.
    (D) The students should read no more than one chapter.

4. (A) He said that the library was open for ten hours.
    (B) We knew how long the library was open.
    (C) Bob spent ten dollars at the library opening.
    (D) He said that we could get into the library at 10:00.

5. (A) Sally was mad about finishing the assignment.
    (B) Sally never finished the math assignment.
    (C) Sally was forced to finish the assignment.
    (D) I finished Sally's assignment.

6. (A) All of a student's courses are electives.
    (B) A student chooses three optional courses after finishing the required courses.
    (C) A student is required to take three electives.
    (D) Finnish is a required course or an elective.

7. (A) Martha discussed whale migration.
    (B) Martha talked to a marine biologist about whale migration.
    (C) Martha wants to take a marine biology seminar.
    (D) Martha wants to be a marine biologist in the summer.

8. (A) The dean listens to the circumstances of complaints.
    (B) The dean never complains about the circumstances.
    (C) The dean always listens to any complaints.
    (D) The dean never hears any complaints.

9. (A) Amy always studied at the same time as Mark.
    (B) Mark studied for the exam before Amy.
    (C) Both Amy and Mark studied hard.
    (D) Amy thought that Mark would study for the exam.

10. (A) Perhaps the building was started last month.
    (B) This month they are definitely starting the building.
    (C) It might be startling to see the building.
    (D) The building probably will begin in a month.

11. (A) What do you think we should do after lunch?
    (B) Aren't you delirious about lunch?
    (C) This lunch really tastes good.
    (D) I don't think this lunch is delicious.

GO ON TO THE NEXT PAGE

PRACTICE TEST THREE

12. (A) He should receive checks for the students on assignment.
     (B) He doesn't know the names of the students doing the assignment.
     (C) He should indicate who has finished the work.
     (D) He checked to see that the students were working on the assignment.

13. (A) It rained unusually hard this year.
     (B) We haven't seen any rain for many years.
     (C) It's been many years since it's rained.
     (D) We don't like this rain.

14. (A) She saw Nick at the time she hit the truck.
     (B) She has a knack of missing trucks all the time.
     (C) She barely avoided the truck.
     (D) When she missed the truck, she swerved for a time.

15. (A) The lawyer sat down with her to watch the news.
     (B) When the lawyer sat down, he broke the chair.
     (C) The news story about the lawyer broke quickly.
     (D) The lawyer told her what had happened.

16. (A) Suzanne was stunned when she saw the dress.
     (B) Suzanne began to dress for the party.
     (C) Suzanne brought a new dish to the party.
     (D) Suzanne purchased an attractive new outfit.

17. (A) It'll cost more to include an additional stop.
     (B) The free agent toured another city.
     (C) The addition of the fee angered the agency.
     (D) In the next city, the agency will feed the tourists.

18. (A) The child was too afraid to remain.
     (B) The child ran into the room because she was frightened.
     (C) The child decided to stay longer in the room.
     (D) The longer she stayed, the more frightened she became.

19. (A) She selected some wide shoes at the mall.
     (B) There's a variety of shoes to choose from at the shopping center.
     (C) You can choose what you want after all.
     (D) There's a wide selection of schools in the fall.

20. (A) He's required to attend the seminar.
     (B) He's still attending the seminar.
     (C) He hasn't attended any seminars.
     (D) He'll attend a seminar later.

GO ON TO THE NEXT PAGE

Part B

<u>Directions:</u> In Part B you will hear short conversations between two speakers. At the end of each conversation, a third person will ask a question about what was said. You will hear each conversation and question about it just one time. Therefore, you must listen carefully to understand what each speaker says. After you hear a conversation and the question about it, read the four possible answers in your test book and decide which <u>one</u> is the best answer to the question you heard. Then, on your answer sheet, find the number of the question and fill in the space that corresponds to the letter of the answer you have chosen.

Look at the following example.

You will hear:

You will read:
(A) The exam was really awful.
(B) It was the worst exam she had ever seen.
(C) It couldn't have been more difficult.
(D) It wasn't that hard.

Sample Answer

Ⓐ Ⓑ Ⓒ ●

From the conversation you learn that the man thought the exam was very difficult and that the woman disagreed with the man. The best answer to the question "What does the woman mean?" is (D), "It wasn't that hard." Therefore, you should choose answer (D).

21. (A) He's reserved in answering the question.
    (B) It's possible to sit anywhere.
    (C) Some of the seats are being saved for others.
    (D) There's only one section of seats.

22. (A) Leave the session.
    (B) Sit down.
    (C) Mind him.
    (D) Conduct the session.

23. (A) He's finished with the dishes.
    (B) He worked on his term paper after finishing the dishes.
    (C) He doesn't like doing his term paper.
    (D) The dishes aren't done yet.

24. (A) That she leave New York with Mike.
    (B) That she go to the airport after work.
    (C) That she ask someone else to take her.
    (D) That she leave tomorrow at noon.

25. (A) He should leave in the morning.
    (B) He should finish the problems before midnight.
    (C) He should work from midnight to morning.
    (D) He shouldn't try to finish everything tonight.

26. (A) The size of the electric bill.
    (B) A problem with the lights.
    (C) Turning in the utility bill.
    (D) Keeping the utility bill high.

PRACTICE TEST THREE

GO ON TO THE NEXT PAGE

27. (A) He's seen the announcement.
    (B) He isn't sure what the announcement means.
    (C) He's uncertain where the lobby is.
    (D) He doesn't know what she's referring to.

28. (A) They haven't finished their work.
    (B) The factory will shut down because it's late.
    (C) They aren't supposed to work at night.
    (D) They should shout about how much they have to do.

29. (A) She's doubtful about the lecture.
    (B) She'll go to the lecture without her watch.
    (C) The worth of the lecture is uncertain.
    (D) She believes the talk will be valuable.

30. (A) Get drinks.
    (B) Watch the game for now.
    (C) Listen to the anthem.
    (D) Finish the game.

31. (A) He doesn't like the idea of bringing a camera.
    (B) Using a camera with sound is a bad idea.
    (C) He doesn't like the sound of the camera.
    (D) He'd like to take some pictures.

32. (A) She and the man are in agreement.
    (B) She'd like to go to the moon.
    (C) She thinks the airplane's flying reasonably high.
    (D) She finds the prices reasonable.

33. (A) He doesn't look like he participates in sports.
    (B) He doesn't like to meet most people.
    (C) It occurred to him that most people aren't athletes.
    (D) He isn't an athlete.

34. (A) The presentation is soon.
    (B) She suggests working on the project at 12:00.
    (C) She'd like to meet the man later today for lunch.
    (D) She'll present her work to the man.

35. (A) He doesn't like the Bahamas.
    (B) He can't make time for a trip to the Bahamas.
    (C) He can't afford the trip.
    (D) He wants to spend his money in the Bahamas.

Part C

Directions: In this part of the test, you will hear short talks and conversations. After each of them, you will be asked some questions. You will hear the talks and conversations and the questions about them just one time. They will not be written out for you. Therefore, you must listen carefully to understand what each speaker says.

After you hear a question, read the four possible answers in your test book and decide which <u>one</u> is the best answer to the question you heard. Then, on your answer sheet,

GO ON TO THE NEXT PAGE

find the number of the question and fill in the space that corresponds to the letter of the answer you have chosen.

Listen to this sample talk.

You will hear:

Now look at the following example.

You will hear: Sample Answer

You will read: (A) Art from America's inner cities.   Ⓐ Ⓑ Ⓒ ●
                (B) Art from the central region of
                    the U.S.
                (C) Art from various urban areas in
                    the U.S.
                (D) Art from rural sections of
                    America.

The best answer to the question "What style of painting is known as American regionalist?" is (D), "Art from rural sections of America." Therefore, you should choose answer (D).

Now look at the next example.

You will hear: Sample Answer

You will read: (A) *American Regionalist.*   Ⓐ Ⓑ ● Ⓓ
                (B) *The Family Farm in Iowa.*
                (C) *American Gothic.*
                (D) *A Serious Couple.*

The best answer to the question "What is the name of Wood's most successful painting?" is (C), *"American Gothic."* Therefore, you should choose answer (C).

36. (A) To write his paper.
    (B) To help him decide on a paper
        topic.
    (C) To teach him about history.
    (D) To discuss history with him.

37. (A) At the beginning of the
        semester.
    (B) Before the start of the semester.
    (C) Near the end of the semester.
    (D) One week after the semester.

38. (A) The American Revolution.
    (B) American Wars.
    (C) The American Automobile.
    (D) American History.

39. (A) The topic's too general.
    (B) He isn't interested in technology.
    (C) He doesn't have enough time.
    (D) Technology has nothing to do
        with American history.

40. (A) A month.
    (B) The semester.
    (C) Seven days.
    (D) A day or two.

41. (A) The purpose of the FCC.
    (B) The relatively rapid
        development of radio.
    (C) Interference from competing
        radio stations.
    (D) The first U.S. radio station.

PRACTICE TEST THREE   GO ON TO THE NEXT PAGE ➤

42. (A) Introduction to Engineering.
    (B) Popular Radio Programs.
    (C) Ethics in Journalism.
    (D) The History of Communications.

43. (A) The many radio stations were highly regulated.
    (B) In 1930 there was only one radio station in the U.S.
    (C) The existing radio stations were totally uncontrolled.
    (D) The FCC was unable to control the radio stations.

44. (A) First Communications Committee.
    (B) First Control Committee.
    (C) Federal Control of Communications.
    (D) Federal Communications Commission.

45. (A) An artist.
    (B) A tour guide.
    (C) An Indian.
    (D) Orville Wright.

46. (A) Several.
    (B) Sixty thousand.
    (C) Sixteen million.
    (D) Millions and millions.

47. (A) The National Air and Space Museum.
    (B) The Museum of Natural History.
    (C) The American History Museum.
    (D) The Smithsonian Arts and Industries Building.

48. (A) The American History Museum.
    (B) The Smithsonian Arts and Industries Building.
    (C) The Washington Museum.
    (D) The National Air and Space Museum.

49. (A) The first thing today.
    (B) After visiting other museums.
    (C) Tomorrow.
    (D) Anytime before leaving Washington, D.C.

50. (A) To the White House.
    (B) To the Smithsonian.
    (C) To the mall.
    (D) To various other museums.

THIS IS THE END OF THE LISTENING COMPREHENSION SECTION OF THE TEST

THE NEXT PART OF THE TEST IS SECTION 2. TURN TO THE
DIRECTIONS FOR SECTION 2 IN YOUR TEST BOOK.
READ THEM, AND BEGIN WORK.
DO NOT READ OR WORK ON ANY OTHER SECTION OF THE TEST.

SECTION 2
STRUCTURE AND WRITTEN EXPRESSION
Time—25 minutes

This section is designed to measure your ability to recognize language that is appropriate for standard written English. There are two types of questions in this section, with special directions for each type.

Directions: Questions 1–15 are incomplete sentences. Beneath each sentence you will see four words or phrases, marked (A), (B), (C), and (D). Choose the one word or phrase that best completes the sentence. Then, on your answer sheet, find the number of the question and fill in the space that corresponds to the letter of the answer you have chosen. Fill in the space so that the letter inside the oval cannot be seen.

Example I   Sample Answer

The president _____ the election   ● ⓑ ⓒ ⓓ
by a landslide.

(A) won
(B) he won
(C) yesterday
(D) fortunately

The sentence should read, "The president won the election by a landslide." Therefore, you should choose answer (A).

Example II   Sample Answer

When _____ the conference?   ⓐ ● ⓒ ⓓ

(A) the doctor attended
(B) did the doctor attend
(C) the doctor will attend
(D) the doctor's attendance

The sentence should read, "When did the doctor attend the conference?" Therefore, you should choose answer (B).

After you read the directions, begin work on the questions.

GO ON TO THE NEXT PAGE

PRACTICE TEST THREE   **71**

1. Overexposure to the sun causes _____ health problems.

   (A) various
   (B) among
   (C) but
   (D) of

2. Birds head south to warmer climates when _____.

   (A) is cold weather
   (B) does cold weather come
   (C) cold weather comes
   (D) comes cold weather

3. The city council is empowered not only to enact new laws, _____ select a new mayor between elections should the need arise.

   (A) and to
   (B) but also to
   (C) and
   (D) so that

4. Drying of meats and vegetables is no longer considered one of _____ of preserving food.

   (A) the ways are useful
   (B) the ways most useful
   (C) the most useful ways
   (D) most are useful ways

5. A giant kind of grass, bamboo may reach a height of 120 feet and _____.

   (A) a diameter of one foot
   (B) its diameter is one foot
   (C) there is a diameter of one foot
   (D) which is a diameter of one foot

6. A thermometer is an instrument that _____ temperature.

   (A) the heat
   (B) having
   (C) does not
   (D) measures

7. Aspirin is used _____ a constriction of the blood vessels.

   (A) the counteraction
   (B) to counteract
   (C) counteract
   (D) counteracting

8. The nuthatch _____ six inches long.

   (A) grows seldom more than
   (B) more than seldom grows
   (C) seldom grows more than
   (D) grows more than seldom

9. Composing more than forty percent of the diet, fats are _____ by the body for energy.

   (A) using specifically
   (B) used specifically
   (C) specific use
   (D) the use specific

10. The sea mammal *medusa* is popularly called a jellyfish because it _____ jelly.

    (A) looks rather like
    (B) looks like rather
    (C) which looks rather like
    (D) which looks like rather

11. Therapists are currently using mental imagery in the hope that it might prove _____ in the treatment of cancer.

    (A) helpful
    (B) for help
    (C) helpfully
    (D) with the help

GO ON TO THE NEXT PAGE

12. By praying outside saloons, throwing rocks in saloon windows, and destroying saloons with her hatchet, _____.

    (A) alcohol was prohibited by Carrie Nation
    (B) Carrie Nation worked to prohibit alcohol
    (C) prohibiting alcohol by Carrie Nation
    (D) Carrie Nation's work for the prohibition of alcohol

13. Somerset Maugham, a novelist, _____ about a restless man's quest for inner understanding in *The Razor's Edge*.

    (A) who wrote this
    (B) who wrote
    (C) when he wrote
    (D) wrote

14. _____ cockroach is the pest most in need of eradication is generally agreed upon by housing authorities everywhere.

    (A) When the
    (B) It is the
    (C) That the
    (D) The

15. _____, the jaguar used to roam freely in the southwestern United States.

    (A) It is now found only in Central and South America
    (B) Now finding in Central and South America
    (C) To be found in Central and South America
    (D) Now found only in Central and South America

Directions: In questions 16–40 each sentence has four underlined words or phrases. The four underlined parts of the sentence are marked (A), (B), (C), and (D). Identify the one underlined word or phrase that must be changed in order for the sentence to be correct. Then, on your answer sheet, find the number of the question and fill in the space that corresponds to the letter of the answer you have chosen.

Example I

The four string on a violin are tuned in fifths.
  A   B   C   D

Sample Answer

(A) ● (C) (D)

The sentence should read, "The four strings on a violin are tuned in fifths." Therefore, you should choose answer (B).

Example II

The research for the book *Roots* taking Alex Haley
      A   B   C
twelve years.
   D

Sample Answer

(A) (B) ● (D)

The sentence should read, "The research for the book *Roots* took Alex Haley twelve years." Therefore, you should choose answer (C).

After you read the directions, begin work on the questions.

PRACTICE TEST THREE

GO ON TO THE NEXT PAGE

16. The <u>larger</u> of the forty-eight <u>continental</u> states <u>in the</u> United States <u>is</u> Texas.
     A   B   C   D

17. According to the experts, <u>genetic</u> inheritance is <u>probability</u> <u>the most</u> important
                                A   B   C
    factor in <u>determining</u> a person's health.
              D

18. The railroad was <u>one</u> of <u>the first</u> <u>methods</u> of transportation to be <u>use</u> extensively in
                  A   B   C   D
    early American history.

19. The National Wildflower Research Center <u>which was</u> <u>established</u> in 1982 by Lady
                                       A   B
    Bird Johnson <u>on sixty acres</u> of land <u>east of</u> Austin.
                   C   D

20. Pioneers <u>on the</u> plains <u>sometimes</u> <u>living</u> in dugouts, sod rooms <u>cut into</u> hillsides.
          A   B   C   D

21. The need <u>to improve</u> technique <u>motivates</u> ballerinas <u>exercising</u> and rehearse for
           A   B   C
    hours <u>daily</u>.
       D

22. <u>While</u> his racing days, racehorse John Henry <u>earned</u> a record $6.5 million, $2.3
 A   B
    million <u>more than</u> his <u>closest</u> competitor.
         C   D

23. <u>Often</u> when the weather is extremely hot, people <u>have</u> very thirsty <u>but</u> are not
 A   B   C
    <u>terribly</u> hungry.
   D

24. The idea <u>that</u> artistic achievements <u>rank</u> in importance with scientific
        A   B
    achievements has been <u>upheld</u> by painters, writers, and <u>musicals</u> for centuries.
                 C   D

25. To <u>improvement</u> the <u>stability</u> of the building, a concrete foundation two <u>feet</u> thick
       A   B   C
    must be <u>installed</u>.
        D

26. In 1784 Benjamin Franklin <u>first suggested</u> daylight savings time as a <u>means</u> of
                         A   B
    <u>cutting</u> down on <u>consumes candles</u>.
   C   D

GO ON TO THE NEXT PAGE ➤

27. An alligator is <u>an animal</u> <u>some</u> like a crocodile, <u>but</u> with a broad, <u>flattened</u> snout.
                   A   B   C   D

28. A new <u>form</u> of cocaine, crack <u>attacks</u> the nervous system, brain, and <u>bodily</u> in a
         A   B   C
<u>sharper</u> fashion than cocaine.
D

29. It <u>has been</u> <u>suggestioned</u> that the battleship "Missouri" be <u>brought</u> back to <u>active</u>
   A   B   C   D
duty, at a cost of $475 million.

30. <u>Into among</u> the five Great Lakes, only Lake Michigan <u>is located</u> <u>entirely</u> within
    A   B   C
the <u>territorial boundaries</u> of the United States.
D

31. Teddy Roosevelt <u>demonstrated</u> his <u>competitive</u> spirit and tireless energy in 1905
                  A   B
<u>whenever</u> <u>he</u> led the Rough Riders up San Juan Hill.
C   D

32. The "Fairness Doctrine" of the FCC <u>requires that</u> radio and television <u>stations</u> give
                                A   B
equal time to <u>opposing sides</u> of <u>issues controversial</u>.
C   D

33. Mary Harris Jones, <u>known</u> as "Mother Jones," was <u>a prominent</u> figure in the
                   A   B
<u>labor movement</u> at the <u>turning</u> of the century.
C   D

34. <u>Consequently</u> the kit fox is <u>an</u> endangered species, wildlife experts in the California
   A   B
desert <u>are using</u> various methods to protect <u>it</u>.
C   D

35. <u>In additions</u> to <u>serving as</u> a member of the President's Cabinet, the Attorney
   A   B
General is <u>the</u> <u>head</u> of the Justice Department.
C   D

36. The narwhal can be easily <u>to recognize</u> by the long <u>spiraled</u> tusk <u>attached to</u> the
                        A   B   C
left side of <u>its</u> head.
D

GO ON TO THE NEXT PAGE

37. The <u>poet</u> Ogden Nash <u>often used</u> a <u>comic</u> style <u>to do</u> a serious point.
      A   B   C   D

38. <u>Much</u> Civil War battles <u>were fought</u> in Virginia than in any <u>other</u> <u>state</u>.
   A   B   C   D

39. <u>It is</u> the role of the National Bureau of Standards to <u>establish</u> accurate
   A   B

    <u>measurements</u> for science, <u>industrial</u>, and commerce.
        C   D

40. On February 20, 1962, "Friendship 7" <u>orbiting</u> the earth in a <u>manned</u> flight <u>that</u>
                             A   B   C

    lasted <u>just under</u> five hours.
          D

THIS IS THE END OF SECTION 2

IF YOU FINISH BEFORE TIME IS CALLED, CHECK YOUR WORK
ON SECTION 2 ONLY.
DO NOT READ OR WORK ON ANY OTHER SECTION OF THE TEST.
THE SUPERVISOR WILL TELL YOU WHEN TO BEGIN
WORK ON SECTION 3.

SECTION 3
VOCABULARY AND READING COMPREHENSION
Time—45 minutes

This section is designed to measure your comprehension of standard written English. There are two types of questions in this section, with special directions for each type.

<u>Directions:</u>   In questions 1–30 each sentence has an underlined word or phrase. Below each sentence are four other words or phrases, marked (A), (B), (C), and (D). You are to choose the <u>one</u> word or phrase that <u>best keeps the meaning</u> of the original sentence if it is substituted for the underlined word or phrase. Then, on your answer sheet, find the number of the question and fill in the space that corresponds to the letter you have chosen. Fill in the space so that the letter inside the oval cannot be seen.

Example   <u>Sample Answer</u>

Both <u>boats</u> and trains are used for   Ⓐ ● Ⓒ Ⓓ
transporting the materials.

(A) planes
(B) ships
(C) canoes
(D) railroads

The best answer is (B) because "Both ships and trains are used for transporting the materials" is closest in meaning to the original sentence. Therefore, you should choose answer (B).

After you read the directions, begin work on the questions.

1. Heterogeneous catalysts are <u>widely</u> used in petroleum production.

    (A) strongly
    (B) extensively
    (C) weightily
    (D) narrowly

2. <u>A messenger</u> was sent to the council with important information.

    (A) An activist
    (B) A career
    (C) An envoy
    (D) A scout

3. In some countries, nuclear power <u>produces</u> up to two-thirds of the necessary electricity.

    (A) makes
    (B) receives
    (C) dissipates
    (D) manages

4. Diffusion occurs at a slower <u>rate</u> in liquids than in gases.

    (A) percentage
    (B) speed
    (C) time
    (D) amount

GO ON TO THE NEXT PAGE

5. A two-thirds majority in Congress is <u>required</u> if a bill is to become law.

   (A) necessary
   (B) desirable
   (C) acquired
   (D) optional

6. The first <u>published</u> article on logarithms, complete with tables, appeared in 1614.

   (A) edited
   (B) noticed
   (C) apparent
   (D) printed

7. Caffeine is a stimulant that was <u>originally</u> produced from plants but now can be made under laboratory conditions.

   (A) first
   (B) appropriately
   (C) often
   (D) only

8. The speed of light is used to measure the <u>vast</u> spaces between stars and planets.

   (A) empty
   (B) huge
   (C) interstellar
   (D) infinite

9. Although Florida is <u>commonly</u> believed to be the southernmost state in the United States, Hawaii really is.

   (A) sporadically
   (B) basically
   (C) generally
   (D) unwaveringly

10. Insects are the most <u>diverse</u> class of animals in number, form, and natural range.

    (A) poetic
    (B) intricate
    (C) varied
    (D) hard working

11. The Sahara, the world's largest desert, <u>extends</u> over 9 million square kilometers.

    (A) spreads
    (B) sits
    (C) presents
    (D) condenses

12. Mental patients are sometimes given the drug chlorpromazine to reduce <u>tension</u>.

    (A) stress
    (B) disease
    (C) pain
    (D) awareness

13. The <u>most secure</u> type of bolt is a deadbolt.

    (A) heaviest
    (B) most costly
    (C) most common
    (D) safest

14. The United States government <u>issues</u> three types of passports: diplomatic, official, and regular.

    (A) orders
    (B) circulates
    (C) retains
    (D) relies on

GO ON TO THE NEXT PAGE

15. Death Valley received its name because of its <u>desolate</u> desert environment.

    (A) sandy
    (B) hot
    (C) barren
    (D) deadly

16. When in Washington, the U.S. President <u>resides at</u> the White House.

    (A) returns to
    (B) resists
    (C) lives in
    (D) sides with

17. The fer-de-lance, a kind of viper, is one of the most <u>poisonous</u> snakes.

    (A) deadly
    (B) vicious
    (C) bad tasting
    (D) unhealthy

18. Carbon monoxide <u>prevents</u> hemoglobin from <u>supplying</u> oxygen to the body.

    (A) discourages
    (B) distracts
    (C) impedes
    (D) excuses

19. There are hundreds of <u>species</u> of eels, some living in fresh water but most living in oceanic waters.

    (A) specialties
    (B) relatives
    (C) kinds
    (D) offspring

20. The gold depository at Fort Knox, Kentucky <u>regularly</u> contains more than $6 billion.

    (A) sometimes
    (B) occasionally
    (C) intermittently
    (D) normally

21. Many Pennsylvania Dutch barns are <u>decorated</u> with hex signs.

    (A) covered
    (B) ornamented
    (C) delighted
    (D) created

22. <u>Domestic</u> cats in the United States are generally classified in ten short-haired breeds and seven long-haired breeds.

    (A) Household
    (B) Friendly
    (C) Trained
    (D) Foreign

23. Exchange rates for most <u>currencies</u> do not float freely.

    (A) newspapers
    (B) securities
    (C) money
    (D) finances

24. The eight survivors <u>subsisted</u> for four days and nights on sea biscuits and mere gulps of water.

    (A) subscribed
    (B) misled
    (C) wandered
    (D) endured

25. On the Farenheit scale, 32 degrees is the freezing point of <u>pure</u> water.

    (A) desalinated
    (B) oceanic
    (C) untainted
    (D) unassimilated

26. Chlorophyll cannot be produced unless the plant is <u>exposed to</u> light.

    (A) raised with
    (B) subjected to
    (C) kept from
    (D) developed with

GO ON TO THE NEXT PAGE

PRACTICE TEST THREE

27. Ice Age fossils from the La Brea tar pits in Los Angeles are now <u>on display</u> in the Natural History Museum in Los Angeles County.

(A) located
(B) on exhibit
(C) under supervision
(D) stored

28. The earliest canoes were made from <u>hollowed</u> tree trunks.

(A) sturdy
(B) burnt
(C) heavy
(D) emptied

29. The <u>background</u> of a painting helps to establish the painting's tone.

(A) setting
(B) return
(C) home
(D) subject

30. The worst <u>flood</u> in the history of the United States occurred in 1927.

(A) storm
(B) deluge
(C) avalanche
(D) circumstance

Directions: In the rest of this section you will read several passages. Each one is followed by several questions about it. For questions 31–60, you are to choose the <u>one</u> best answer, (A), (B), (C), or (D), to each question. Then, on your answer sheet, find <u>the</u> number of the question and fill in the space that corresponds to the letter of the answer you have chosen.

Answer all questions following a passage on the basis of what is <u>stated</u> or <u>implied</u> in that passage.

Read the following passage:

John Quincy Adams, who served as the sixth president of the United States from 1825 to 1829, is today recognized for his masterful statesmanship and diplomacy. He dedicated his life to public service, both in the presidency and in the various other political offices he held. Throughout his political career he demonstrated his unswerving belief in freedom of speech, the anti-slavery cause, and the right of Americans to be free from European and Asian domination.

Example I

To what did John Quincy Adams devote his life?

Sample Answer

(A) Improving his personal life
(B) Serving the public
(C) Increasing his fortune
(D) Working on his private business

According to the passage, John Quincy Adams "dedicated his life to public service." Therefore, you should choose answer (B).

GO ON TO THE NEXT PAGE

Example II

The passage implies that John
Quincy Adams held

(A) no political offices
(B) only one political office
(C) exactly two political offices
(D) at least three political offices

The passage states that John Quincy Adams served in "the presidency and various other political offices." Therefore, you should choose answer (D).

After you read the directions, begin work on the questions.

Questions 31–35

Geographically, California's diversity is breathtaking, and the state's coastline from north to south is no exception. Measuring 840 miles in length, the coast consists of the rugged cliffs of the Coast Ranges in the north and wide sandy beaches in the south. Along the coastline there are two major harbors, one in the north at San Francisco, the other in the south at San Diego. Near Humboldt and Monterey are smaller natural harbors.

31. The topic of this passage is

(A) how the state of California is divided into north and south
(B) the variations in California's coastal geography
(C) the breathtaking beauty of California
(D) the exceptions in coastal geography

32. According to the passage, what measures 840 miles in length?

(A) The California coastline
(B) The Coast Ranges
(C) The rugged cliffs
(D) The exceptional part of northern California

33. The Coast Ranges are

(A) flat, sandy areas on the coast of California
(B) found in southern California
(C) a series of mountains
(D) hundreds of miles north of the cliffs

34. It is implied in the passage that northern California

(A) has more beaches than southern California
(B) is roughly the same as southern California
(C) has fewer major harbors than southern California
(D) has a substantially different coastline from southern California

35. According to the passage, where are the major harbors located in California?

(A) In San Diego
(B) Only in northern California
(C) Near Humboldt and Monterey
(D) In the north and in the south

GO ON TO THE NEXT PAGE

Questions 36–41

The invention of the phonograph happened quite by accident. Thomas Edison moved to Menlo Park, New Jersey, in 1876, where he established an industrial research laboratory. There Edison worked on a carbon telephone transmitter to improve the existing Bell system. In that laboratory a year later Edison invented the phonograph while trying to improve a telegraph repeater. He attached a telephone diaphragm to the needle in the telegraph repeater to produce a recording that could be played back. After some improvements to the machine, he recited "Mary Had a Little Lamb" and played the recognizable reproduction of his voice back to an astonished audience.

36. What is the best title for the passage?

(A) Thomas Edison's Many Inventions
(B) Improvements in the Telephone and Telegraph
(C) The History of Menlo Park
(D) A Surprise Invention

37. According to the passage, the invention of the phonograph

(A) was quite unplanned
(B) was Edison's principal project
(C) was surprising to no one
(D) took many years

38. In what year did the invention of the phonograph occur?

(A) 1876
(B) 1877
(C) 1878
(D) The article does not say.

39. According to the passage, how was the phonograph made?

(A) With a telephone needle and a recorder
(B) From a recording of a telegraph
(C) With only a telegraph repeater
(D) From a combination of telephone and telegraph parts

40. According to the passage, how did Edison test his new invention?

(A) He made improvements to the machine.
(B) He used a carbon transmitter.
(C) He read a children's rhyme.
(D) He reproduced the audience's voice.

41. According to the passage, how did people feel when they heard Edison's rendition of "Mary Had a Little Lamb"?

(A) Perplexed
(B) Amazed
(C) Aggravated
(D) Detached

GO ON TO THE NEXT PAGE

Questions 42–47

Distillation, the process of separating the elements of a solution, is widely used in industry today. The two most common methods of distillation are fractional distillation, used in the preparation of alcoholic beverages, and flash distillation, used for the conversion of ocean water to fresh water.

In fractional distillation a mixture is separated into its various component parts by boiling. This method makes use of the fact that different elements boil at varying temperatures. For example, alcohol has a considerably lower boiling temperature than water: the boiling temperature of water is 212 degrees and the boiling temperature of alcohol is 172 degrees. Thus, when a mixture of alcohol and water is heated, the alcohol vaporizes more quickly than the water. The distillate is collected and the process is repeated until the desired purity has been achieved.

Flash distillation does not require high temperatures but instead is based on pressure. In this process, a liquid that is to be separated is forced from a compartment kept under high pressure into a compartment kept at a lower pressure. When a liquid moves into the low-pressure chamber, it suddenly vaporizes, and the vapor is then condensed into distillate.

42. According to the passage, what makes fractional distillation occur?

(A) Time
(B) Pressure
(C) Heat
(D) Water

43. According to the passage, fractional distillation can occur only if

(A) one element is at a higher pressure than the other
(B) the elements of the solution have different boiling temperatures
(C) the solution is forced from a compartment at one temperature into a compartment at another temperature
(D) the solution to be distilled is completely pure

44. Which of the following statements about boiling temperatures is true?

(A) All elements have the same boiling temperature.
(B) Water boils at a lower temperature than alcohol.
(C) Any solution containing water boils at 212 degrees.
(D) Water does not boil at as low a temperature as alcohol.

45. According to the passage, in the flash distillation process, what causes the liquid to vaporize?

(A) The pressure on the liquid is suddenly changed.
(B) The liquid changes compartments.
(C) The addition of sea water to a solution causes a chemical change to occur.
(D) There is a rapid increase in the pressure on the liquid.

GO ON TO THE NEXT PAGE

46. Which of the following processes would probably involve distillation?

   (A) Adding a new substance to a mixture
   (B) Dividing a pure element into smaller quantities
   (C) Mixing two elements together to form a new solution
   (D) Removing impurities from a solution

47. The main purpose of this passage is to

   (A) explain how salt water can be turned into fresh water
   (B) give an example of fractional distillation
   (C) describe a scientific process
   (D) discuss the boiling temperatures of various liquids

Questions 48–55

The Indian cliff dwellings of the southwestern United States are a source of interest and mystery for archeologists. Located in the Four Corners area of the U.S., where Colorado, Utah, Arizona, and New Mexico meet, the cliff dwellings were constructed during the Great Pueblo period, from approximately 1050 to 1300. The cliff dwellings are whole series of contiguous rooms built in layers into the sides of cliffs. The sleeping rooms of the cliff dwellings were very tiny, often only one to two meters wide and little more than one meter high, and they were built in complexes of up to several hundred rooms together. The front rooms of the complexes were considerably larger. These larger rooms were apparently the rooms where daily life took place.

When the cliff dwellings were first found by explorers, they had been abandoned. Archeologists today are uncertain as to when or why they were abandoned and where the inhabitants went. There is some evidence, however, that the inhabitants left the cliff dwellings near the end of the thirteenth century because of a serious drought that is known to have occurred in the area from 1276 to 1299. Archeologists believe that the inhabitants could have left the cliff dwellings to move southwest and southeast. Today the descendants of the cliff dwellers are probably members of the Indian tribes of that area.

48. Which of the following is the best topic for this passage?

   (A) The Great Pueblo period
   (B) A description of the Indian cliff dwellings
   (C) What is known and unknown about the cliff dwellings
   (D) The Four Corners area of the United States

49. Why did the Four Corners area receive its name?

   (A) The area is a square with four corners.
   (B) The cliff dwellings in the area each have four corners.
   (C) The Great Pueblos are four-cornered.
   (D) The corners of four states meet there.

GO ON TO THE NEXT PAGE

50. According to the passage, when were the cliff dwellings built?

   (A) During the Great Pueblo period
   (B) After the drought
   (C) Sometime before 1050
   (D) At the same time that the explorers found them

51. According to the passage, what size were the sleeping chambers?

   (A) Wide
   (B) Small
   (C) High
   (D) Large

52. According to the passage, what were the cliff dwellings like when the explorers first found them?

   (A) Thriving
   (B) Full of daily life
   (C) Empty
   (D) In a state of drought

53. According to the passage, what do archeologists believe caused the cliff dwellers to abandon their homes?

   (A) A lack of food
   (B) Warfare with neighboring tribes
   (C) A desire to find a safer location
   (D) A shortage of water

54. According to the passage, which of the following are the authorities certain about?

   (A) Why the cliff dwellers abandoned their homes
   (B) That a drought occurred in the Four Corners area from 1276 to 1299
   (C) Where the inhabitants of the cliff dwellings went
   (D) When the cliff dwellers abandoned their homes

55. Which of the following is NOT discussed in the passage?

   (A) The lifestyle of the cliff dwellers
   (B) The size of the cliff dwellings
   (C) The mystery surrounding the abandonment of the cliff dwellings
   (D) The location of the cliff dwellings

GO ON TO THE NEXT PAGE

Questions 56–60

At first glance it might seem that a true artist is a solitary toiler in possession of a unique talent that differentiates him from the rest of society. But after further reflection it is quite apparent that the artist is a product of the society in which he toils rather than an entity removed from that society. The genius of an artist is really a measure of the artist's ability to work within the framework imposed by society, to make use of the resources provided by society, and, most important, to mirror a society's values. It is society that imposes a structure on the artist, and the successful artist must work within this framework. Societies have found various methods to support and train their artists, be it the Renaissance system of royal support of the sculptors and painters of the period or the Japanese tradition of passing artistic knowledge from father to son. The artist is also greatly affected by the physical resources of his society. The medium chosen by the artist is a reflection not only of the artist's perception of aesthetic beauty but of resources that society has to supply. After all, wood carvings come from societies with forests, woven woolen rugs come from societies of shepherds, shell jewelry comes from societies near oceans. Finally, the artist must reflect the values, both aesthetic and moral, of the society in which he toils. The idea of beauty changes from society to society, as seen in the oft cited example of Rubens' rounded women versus today's gamin-like sylphs, and the artist must serve as a mirror of his society's measure of perfection. And society's moral values must equally be reflected in art if it is to be universally accepted.

56. What does the passage mainly discuss?

(A) The effect of the artist on society
(B) The role of an artist in improving society
(C) The relation between an artist and society
(D) The structure of society

57. The author thinks that an artist is

(A) separate from society
(B) a part of society
(C) differentiated from society
(D) an entity removed from society

58. According to the passage, which of the following is NOT a way that society imposes its structure on an artist?

(A) Society has found ways to train and support its artists.
(B) Society provides physical resources to an artist.
(C) Society imposes its values on the artist.
(D) Society allows the artist to use his unique talent to lead a solitary life.

GO ON TO THE NEXT PAGE

59. Which of the following physical resources of art is NOT mentioned in the passage?

(A) Stone
(B) Wood
(C) Wool
(D) Shell

60. The example of Rubens' women is used to show that the artist

(A) has been supplied by society
(B) makes use of society's physical resources
(C) reflects society's aesthetic values
(D) reflects society's moral values

THIS IS THE END OF SECTION 3

IF YOU FINISH BEFORE TIME IS CALLED, CHECK YOUR WORK
ON SECTION 3 ONLY.
DO NOT READ OR WORK ON ANY OTHER SECTION OF THE TEST.

PRACTICE TEST THREE

TEST OF WRITTEN ENGLISH: ESSAY QUESTION
Time—30 minutes

Some educators believe that to graduate from a university a student should study courses from a wide variety of subjects. Other educators believe that it is better for a university graduate to have a strong specialization. Discuss the advantages of each position. Then indicate which position you think is better and justify your response.

Write your answer on the answer sheet for the Test of Written English, Practice Test Three, on pages 177–178.

PRACTICE TEST FOUR

SECTION 1
LISTENING COMPREHENSION

In this section of the test, you will have an opportunity to demonstrate your ability to understand spoken English. There are three parts in this section, with special directions for each part.

Part A

Directions: For each question in Part A, you will hear a short sentence. Each sentence will be spoken just one time. The sentences you hear will not be written out for you. Therefore, you must listen carefully to understand what the speaker says.

After you hear a sentence, read the four choices in your test book, marked (A), (B), (C), and (D), and decide which one is closest in meaning to the sentence you heard. Then, on your answer sheet, find the number of the question and fill in the space that corresponds to the letter of the answer you have chosen. Fill in the space so the letter inside the oval cannot be seen.

Example I   Sample Answer

You will hear: ●
                                                                            Ⓑ
You will read: (A) John outran the others.   Ⓒ
                  (B) John was the fastest hunter in   Ⓓ
                      the chase.
                  (C) John wasn't the slowest in the
                      race.
                  (D) John was the last runner to
                      finish the race.

The speaker said, "John was the fastest runner in the race." Sentence (A), "John outran the others," is closest in meaning to the sentence you heard. Therefore, you should choose answer (A).

Example II   Sample Answer

You will hear: Ⓐ
                                                                            Ⓑ
You will read: (A) Could you help me use the rest?   ●
                  (B) Do you mind using the other   Ⓓ
                      desk?
                  (C) Would you mind helping me
                      carry this piece of furniture?
                  (D) If you move my desk, I'll help
                      you with your work.

The speaker said, "Could you help me move my desk?" Sentence (C), "Would you mind helping me carry this piece of furniture?" is closest in meaning to the sentence you heard. Therefore, you should choose answer (C).

GO ON TO THE NEXT PAGE ▶

1. (A) I don't think the bus is expensive.
   (B) I think it's expensive to take the bus to the city.
   (C) Do you agree that the bus costs a lot?
   (D) Don't you think that this city's expensive?

2. (A) If she moved her desk, she couldn't see the blackboard.
   (B) Before she moved her desk, she couldn't see the blackboard.
   (C) She wanted to move her desk, so she looked at the blackboard.
   (D) She moved so far that the blackboard was out of sight.

3. (A) This class isn't very important to me.
   (B) Nothing at all is important to me.
   (C) This class could be more important to me.
   (D) This class is extremely important to me.

4. (A) I'm not sure if this assignment is difficult.
   (B) Is this assignment very difficult?
   (C) I think this assignment is rather easy.
   (D) This assignment is hard.

5. (A) She should let her car be repaired.
   (B) The mechanic has left for the day.
   (C) Her car has been left with the mechanic.
   (D) The mechanic should leave her in the car.

6. (A) How long do you think it'll take to finish?
   (B) I'll remain no matter how much time we need to finish.
   (C) Whenever we stay, it takes a long time.
   (D) How do we know if it takes a long time to complete?

7. (A) I believe that she didn't take the money.
   (B) It was hard for her to insist that she didn't do it.
   (C) In spite of what she says, it appears she stole the money.
   (D) Although she insisted, she didn't take the money.

8. (A) Mark never works on his biology experiments alone.
   (B) Mark always works with Rita before he goes to the biology lab.
   (C) Mark's working on biology now, and so is Rita.
   (D) When Mark works in the biology lab, he reads.

9. (A) Linda's role in law school is uncertain for next semester.
   (B) Linda will graduate from law school next semester.
   (C) Linda has plans, so she can't attend law school next semester.
   (D) Linda will be a law student when school starts again.

10. (A) He typed every single word of the lecture.
    (B) He didn't understand that the lecture was to be taped.
    (C) I need the tape to listen to the lecture again.
    (D) I'm glad that the lecturer didn't understand a word.

GO ON TO THE NEXT PAGE

11. (A) Denise finished the problems last.
    (B) Denise was instructed to complete the math assignment.
    (C) It was a problem to finish the math.
    (D) Denise told the students to do the math problems.

12. (A) She stored several cartons of books in a closet.
    (B) She found herself in a closet looking for books.
    (C) She located some lost books in a closet.
    (D) She missed the cartons of books in the closet.

13. (A) She couldn't have said anything.
    (B) She said all that she could.
    (C) She couldn't have said that.
    (D) She must have said more.

14. (A) Alice refunded the money to the salesman.
    (B) The salesman refused to give Alice her money.
    (C) Alice was mad when the salesman refused her money.
    (D) The salesman returned Alice's money.

15. (A) No one plays the piano as well as Eric.
    (B) Eric can't play the piano very well.
    (C) Eric's the only one who plays the piano.
    (D) Others play the piano better than Eric.

16. (A) That outline will take no more than two hours.
    (B) He should need more than two hours to complete the outline.
    (C) After he finishes the outline, he'll work for two hours.
    (D) His plans for working were interrupted by the outline.

17. (A) Mr. Milton pointed to the dean of the college.
    (B) The dean of the college pointed out Mr. Milton.
    (C) Mr. Milton had an appointment with the dean of the college.
    (D) Mr. Milton received a new position a year ago.

18. (A) Before you depart, look for a job at the employment office.
    (B) Go to the employment office to learn about part-time employment.
    (C) He's looking for a part-time office job.
    (D) The next office is the place to find a job.

19. (A) I'm surprised that he didn't tell you the truth.
    (B) I think that he wanted to lie down.
    (C) He thought that he could lie to you.
    (D) He could think if he would lie down.

20. (A) You should notice when your landlord comes to your apartment.
    (B) You must move out of your apartment in thirty days.
    (C) One month before you leave your apartment, you must inform the landlord.
    (D) If you move out of your apartment, the landlord will notice.

GO ON TO THE NEXT PAGE ▶

Part B

<u>Directions:</u>   In Part B you will hear short conversations between two speakers. At the end of each conversation, a third person will ask a question about what was said. You will hear each conversation and question about it just one time. Therefore, you must listen carefully to understand what each speaker says. After you hear a conversation and the question about it, read the four possible answers in your test book and decide which <u>one</u> is the best answer to the question you heard. Then, on your answer sheet, find the number of the question and fill in the space that corresponds to the letter of the answer you have chosen.

Look at the following example.

You will hear:

You will read: (A) The exam was really awful.
(B) It was the worst exam she had ever seen.
(C) It couldn't have been more difficult.
(D) ·It wasn't that hard.

<u>Sample Answer</u>

Ⓐ
Ⓑ
Ⓒ
●

From the conversation you learn that the man thought the exam was very difficult and that the woman disagreed with the man. The best answer to the question "What does the woman mean?" is (D), "It wasn't that hard." Therefore, you should choose answer (D).

21. (A) In a bus terminal.
(B) In a tourist agency.
(C) At an airport ticket counter.
(D) At a train station.

22. (A) Ten dollars was too much to pay for perfume.
(B) It was unfortunate that she didn't like the perfume.
(C) Fortunately, she got the perfume for ten dollars.
(D) She didn't have enough money to buy the perfume.

23. (A) The plants need more water today.
(B) The plants don't need to be watered.
(C) Yesterday's watering was insufficient.
(D) He thinks he should water the plants.

24. (A) Paul never likes to play tennis.
(B) Paul's unable to play tennis with them.
(C) Paul isn't a very good tennis player.
(D) Paul is in town for a game of tennis.

25. (A) She believes the cost was reasonable.
(B) The cost was unbelievably low.
(C) She believes she'll stay overnight.
(D) The cost was extremely high.

26. (A) Perhaps she left the checks in her suitcase.
(B) He doesn't know why she's looking in her suitcase.
(C) Maybe the checks are in her purse.
(D) She could've left her purse in the suitcase.

PRACTICE TEST FOUR

GO ON TO THE NEXT PAGE

27. (A) If Eric wants to play basketball.
    (B) If Eric's walking to the basketball game.
    (C) If Eric's hurt.
    (D) If Eric's uncle's playing basketball.

28. (A) Both shirts are made exactly the same.
    (B) It doesn't matter which shirt he gets.
    (C) He shouldn't get either one.
    (D) She doesn't like either shirt.

29. (A) If the car ran out of gas.
    (B) If the car will start.
    (C) Where the gas station is.
    (D) If she should send a check to the service station.

30. (A) Someone talked out loud.
    (B) No one said much of anything.
    (C) The meeting seemed long to everyone.
    (D) A lot of people were talking at once.

31. (A) He thinks the housing deadline hasn't passed.
    (B) He's accepting the housing that's been offered.
    (C) He doesn't have a place to stay.
    (D) He supposes that his application's been accepted.

32. (A) She thinks the homework's easy.
    (B) She doesn't know about the assignment.
    (C) She's worked hard on her biology homework.
    (D) The homework was due yesterday.

33. (A) She spent a lot of time finding the bracelet.
    (B) It wasn't a difficult project.
    (C) The bracelet was hard to make.
    (D) It wasn't worth the time it took.

34. (A) He didn't read Stan's article.
    (B) He read the article when it appeared in the paper.
    (C) He helped Stan with the article.
    (D) Stan read the article in the school paper.

35. (A) He's disappointed about the promotion.
    (B) He made some extra motions.
    (C) He's heard a lot of static.
    (D) He's very pleased.

Part C

Directions: In this part of the test, you will hear short talks and conversations. After each of them, you will be asked some questions. You will hear the talks and conversations and the questions about them just one time. They will not be written out for you. Therefore, you must listen carefully to understand what each speaker says.

After you hear a question, read the four possible answers in your test book and decide which one is the best answer to the question you heard. Then, on your answer sheet, find the number of the question and fill in the space that corresponds to the letter of the answer you have chosen.

94 PRACTICE TEST FOUR

GO ON TO THE NEXT PAGE

Listen to this sample talk.

You will hear:

Now look at the following example.

You will hear: Sample Answer

You will read: (A) Art from America's inner cities.   Ⓐ
                 (B) Art from the central region of   Ⓑ
                       the U.S.   ©
                 (C) Art from various urban areas in   ●
                       the U.S.
                 (D) Art from rural sections of
                       America.

The best answer to the question "What style of painting is known as American regionalist?" is (D), "Art from rural sections of America." Therefore, you should choose answer (D).

Now look at the next example.

You will hear: Sample Answer

You will read: (A) *American Regionalist.*   Ⓐ
                 (B) *The Family Farm in Iowa.*   Ⓑ
                 (C) *American Gothic.*   ●
                 (D) *A Serious Couple.*   Ⓓ

The best answer to the question "What is the name of Wood's most successful painting?" is (C), "*American Gothic.*" Therefore, you should choose answer (C).

36. (A) Two students.
     (B) Two professors.
     (C) Two sociologists.
     (D) Two lecturers.

37. (A) She wants his opinion of
            sociologists.
     (B) She wants to hear him lecture.
     (C) She wants to know about a
            course he took.
     (D) She wants to meet Professor
            Patterson.

38. (A) A social studies seminar.
     (B) A beginning sociology course.
     (C) Introduction to Psychology.
     (D) An advanced sociology lecture.

39. (A) A course where the professor
            lectures.
     (B) A course where the students
            just listen and take notes.
     (C) A course with Professor
            Patterson.
     (D) A course where the students
            take part in discussion.

40. (A) She thinks it'll be boring.
     (B) She doesn't want to take it.
     (C) It sounds good to her.
     (D) She'd prefer a course with
            more student participation.

GO ON TO THE NEXT PAGE

PRACTICE TEST FOUR   **95**

41. (A) The Development of Science and Technology.
    (B) Introduction to Geology.
    (C) American History.
    (D) World Geography.

42. (A) A woodcarving business.
    (B) A lumber business.
    (C) A construction business.
    (D) A jewelry business.

43. (A) During the construction of a sawmill.
    (B) After prospectors had arrived.
    (C) Sometime after Sutter's death.
    (D) Before Sutter had the rights to the land.

44. (A) Increased prosperity.
    (B) A large share of gold.
    (C) A healthier lumber business.
    (D) Little or nothing.

45. (A) To show what a terrible life John Sutter had.
    (B) To show the folly of trying to develop a business.
    (C) To show the effect that the discovery of gold has on individuals.
    (D) To show that the development of the West happened partly by chance.

46. (A) Fire damage to some apartments.
    (B) How to prevent fires.
    (C) An apartment fire and what one can learn from it.
    (D) An early morning news story.

47. (A) One was damaged more severely than some others.
    (B) All the apartments were completely destroyed.
    (C) There was one thousand dollars of damage.
    (D) All twenty apartments suffered some damage.

48. (A) They were killed.
    (B) They were taken to the hospital.
    (C) The damage to the apartments was more serious than the harm to the residents.
    (D) They weren't frightened.

49. (A) Call the fire department.
    (B) Rush to the hospital.
    (C) Listen for a smoke alarm.
    (D) Have an alarm and extinguisher in good condition.

50. (A) It can be used to put out a fire.
    (B) It'll give a warning that a fire has started.
    (C) It'll notify the fire department.
    (D) It's necessary for use with a fire extinguisher.

THIS IS THE END OF THE LISTENING COMPREHENSION SECTION OF THE TEST

THE NEXT PART OF THE TEST IS SECTION 2. TURN TO THE
DIRECTIONS FOR SECTION 2 IN YOUR TEST BOOK.
READ THEM, AND BEGIN WORK.
DO NOT READ OR WORK ON ANY OTHER SECTION OF THE TEST.

STOP STOP STOP STOP STOP STOP STOP

SECTION 2
STRUCTURE AND WRITTEN EXPRESSION
Time—25 minutes

This section is designed to measure your ability to recognize language that is appropriate for standard written English. There are two types of questions in this section, with special directions for each type.

Directions: Questions 1–15 are incomplete sentences. Beneath each sentence you will see four words or phrases, marked (A), (B), (C), and (D). Choose the one word or phrase that best completes the sentence. Then, on your answer sheet, find the number of the question and fill in the space that corresponds to the letter of the answer you have chosen. Fill in the space so that the letter inside the oval cannot be seen.

Example I

The president _____ the election by a landslide.

(A) won
(B) he won
(C) yesterday
(D) fortunately

Sample Answer

● Ⓐ
Ⓑ
Ⓒ
Ⓓ

The sentence should read, "The president won the election by a landslide." Therefore, you should choose answer (A).

Example II

When _____ the conference?

(A) the doctor attended
(B) did the doctor attend
(C) the doctor will attend
(D) the doctor's attendance

Sample Answer

Ⓐ
● Ⓑ
Ⓒ
Ⓓ

The sentence should read, "When did the doctor attend the conference?" Therefore, you should choose answer (B).

After you read the directions, begin work on the questions.

1. The electric eel uses its electric shock to capture food and _____.

   (A) for protection
   (B) protect itself
   (C) protecting itself
   (D) it protects itself

2. _____ anti-trust laws did not exist in the U.S., there would not be as much competition in certain industries.

   (A) So
   (B) If
   (C) For
   (D) Also

PRACTICE TEST FOUR

GO ON TO THE NEXT PAGE ➤

3. In 1885 photography changed dramatically _____ introduced paper-based film.

   (A) Eastman
   (B) when was
   (C) when it was
   (D) when Eastman

4. A bat will often spend the daylight hours _____ upside down in a tree or cave.

   (A) hanging
   (B) which hangs
   (C) that is
   (D) hangs

5. Geomorphology is the study of the changes that _____ on the surface of the earth.

   (A) taking place
   (B) takes place
   (C) take place
   (D) they take place

6. A hero of the war of 1812, _____ President of the United States.

   (A) Andrew Jackson later became
   (B) that Andrew Jackson later became
   (C) who was Andrew Jackson
   (D) later became Andrew Jackson

7. _____ jellies, jams are made by retaining the pulp with the fruit juice.

   (A) No likeness to
   (B) Not alike
   (C) Unlike
   (D) Dislike

8. An elephant can lift _____ a ton with its tusks.

   (A) so much that
   (B) them
   (C) most
   (D) as much as

9. In medieval times _____ his enemy to fight by throwing down his gauntlet.

   (A) the challenge
   (B) a man made a challenge
   (C) a man challenged
   (D) his challenge

10. Rarely _____ acorns until the trees are more than twenty years old.

    (A) when oak trees bear
    (B) oak trees that bear
    (C) do oak trees bear
    (D) oak trees bear

11. The Andromeda Nebula, _____ more than two million light years away, can be seen from the northern hemisphere.

    (A) a galaxy
    (B) is a galaxy
    (C) a galaxy is
    (D) a galaxy which

12. The closer to one of the earth's poles, the greater _____ gravitational force.

    (A) is
    (B) the
    (C) has
    (D) it has

13. Baboons eat a variety of foods, _____ eggs, fruits, grass, insects, plant leaves, and roots.

    (A) they include
    (B) among them are
    (C) among
    (D) including

GO ON TO THE NEXT PAGE ➤

14. The flamingo uses its bill _____ feeding to filter mud and water from the tiny plants and animals it finds in shallow ponds.

    (A) when
    (B) is
    (C) that it is
    (D) was

15. The first nuclear-powered ship in the world, "The Nautilus," _____ by the U.S. Navy in 1954.

    (A) when it was launched
    (B) that was launched
    (C) was launched
    (D) launched

Directions: In questions 16–40 each sentence has four underlined words or phrases. The four underlined parts of the sentence are marked (A), (B), (C), and (D). Identify the one underlined word or phrase that must be changed in order for the sentence to be correct. Then, on your answer sheet, find the number of the question and fill in the space that corresponds to the letter of the answer you have chosen.

Example I   Sample Answer

The four string on a violin are tuned in fifths.
A   B   C   D

The sentence should read, "The four strings on a violin are tuned in fifths." Therefore, you should choose answer (B).

Example II   Sample Answer

The research for the book *Roots* taking Alex Haley
    A   B   C

twelve years.
    D

The sentence should read, "The research for the book *Roots* took Alex Haley twelve years." Therefore, you should choose answer (C).

After you read the directions, begin work on the questions.

16. The winter storm that raced through the area for the last two day moved east
                        A   B   C   D
    today.

17. In the 1800's botanist Asa Gray worked to describe and classifying the plants found
                    A   B   C   D
    in North America.

GO ON TO THE NEXT PAGE ➤

18. Bryce Canyon National Park, where <u>is there</u> <u>oddly shaped</u> and magnificently
    A B

    colored rock <u>formations</u>, is located in <u>southern</u> Utah.
    C D

19. <u>After</u> <u>talks</u> in Copenhagen yesterday, <u>the</u> Secretary of State <u>returning</u> to
    A B C D
    Washington.

20. Lava, <u>rock</u> fragments, and <u>gaseous</u> may <u>all</u> <u>erupt</u> from a volcano.
    A B C D

21. <u>Many of</u> the characters <u>portrayed</u> by writer Joyce Carol Oates <u>is</u> <u>mentally</u> ill.
    A B C D

22. The two <u>types of</u> nucleic acids, <u>known</u> as DNA and RNA, <u>are</u> not <u>the alike</u>.
    A B C D

23. <u>The 1890's</u> <u>in</u> America were known <u>as</u> <u>a</u> Gay Nineties.
    A B C D

24. The classification of a dinosaur <u>as</u> either saurischian <u>nor</u> ornithischian <u>depends on</u>
    A B C

    the structure of <u>the hip</u>.
    D

25. An octopus has three hearts <u>to pump</u> blood <u>throughout</u> <u>their</u> body.
    A B C D

26. Of <u>all the</u> states <u>in the</u> United States, Rhode Island <u>is</u> <u>a</u> smallest.
    A B C D

27. <u>Studies</u> show <u>that the</u> new strategy is not <u>so</u> effective as the <u>previous</u> one.
    A B C D

28. <u>Most</u> newspapers depend <u>on</u> the wire services <u>from</u> their international
    A B C

    <u>stories and photographs</u>.
    D

29. <u>The</u> new system <u>responds</u> <u>at</u> seconds to <u>any</u> emergency.
    A B C D

30. Landscape <u>painting</u> was <u>a dominant</u> art <u>forms</u> <u>during</u> much of the nineteenth
    A B C D
    century.

31. Balloons have been used in <u>various wars</u> not only to direct artillery fire and report
    A

    troop <u>movements</u> <u>however</u> to carry bombs and <u>protect against</u> low-flying planes.
    B C D

GO ON TO THE NEXT PAGE

32. Cartilage <u>covers</u> <u>the ends</u> of bones helps <u>to protect</u> the joints <u>from</u> wear and tear.
               A   B   C   D

33. The Alaskan malamute, <u>used</u> extensively <u>for pulling</u> sleds, is <u>closely</u> related <u>about</u>
                        A   B   C   D
the wolf.

34. The General Agreement on Tariffs and Trades (GATT) is an <u>international</u> agreement
                                                     A
<u>designing</u> to increase trade <u>among</u> <u>member nations</u>.
    B   C   D

35. In a corporation the <u>approval</u> of a majority of stockholders may be <u>required</u> before
                         A   B
<u>a major</u> decision can be <u>done</u>.
   C   D

36. Death Valley <u>is</u> 130 miles <u>length</u> and <u>no more</u> <u>than</u> 14 miles wide.
             A   B   C   D

37. The theory of natural selection <u>is used</u> to explain <u>which</u> animals of a species will
                                A   B
die <u>prematurely</u> and which will <u>survival</u>.
       C   D

38. <u>Almost</u> one-half of <u>those</u> taking <u>specialized</u> courses last year were taking
   A   B   C
self-improvement <u>course</u>.
            D

39. Richard Gatling, an <u>invention</u> best known for the development of the Gatling Gun,
                A
<u>actually</u> put <u>most of</u> his effort into improving <u>agricultural</u> methods.
   B   C   D

40. Dorothea Dix worked <u>extensively</u> <u>during the</u> second half of the nineteenth century
                      A   B
<u>to improve conditions</u> in mental health facilities and <u>the</u> prisons.
        C   D

THIS IS THE END OF SECTION 2

IF YOU FINISH BEFORE TIME IS CALLED, CHECK YOUR WORK
ON SECTION 2 ONLY.
DO NOT READ OR WORK ON ANY OTHER SECTION OF THE TEST.
THE SUPERVISOR WILL TELL YOU WHEN TO BEGIN
WORK ON SECTION 3.

SECTION 3
VOCABULARY AND READING COMPREHENSION
Time—45 minutes

This section is designed to measure your comprehension of standard written English. There are two types of questions in this section, with special directions for each type.

Directions: In questions 1–30 each sentence has an underlined word or phrase. Below each sentence are four other words or phrases, marked (A), (B), (C), and (D). You are to choose the one word or phrase that best keeps the meaning of the original sentence if it is substituted for the underlined word or phrase. Then, on your answer sheet, find the number of the question and fill in the space that corresponds to the letter you have chosen. Fill in the space so that the letter inside the oval cannot be seen.

Example   Sample Answer

Both boats and trains are used for   Ⓐ
transporting the materials.   ●
                                                                              Ⓒ
(A) planes   Ⓓ
(B) ships
(C) canoes
(D) railroads

The best answer is (B) because "Both ships and trains are used for transporting the materials" is closest in meaning to the original sentence. Therefore, you should choose answer (B).

After you read the directions, begin work on the questions.

1. When calcium carbonate crystallizes from a solution, limestone is formed.

    (A) made
    (B) framed
    (C) destroyed
    (D) outlined

2. In a hot air balloon, the altitude is determined by the amount of fuel fed to the burner.

    (A) height
    (B) speed
    (C) length
    (D) magnitude

3. Ralph Nader headed the organization called Public Citizen, Inc. from 1971 to 1980.

    (A) moved
    (B) directed
    (C) turned
    (D) toiled for

4. The harp, with up to 47 strings, produces the most tones of any stringed instrument.

    (A) noise
    (B) melodies
    (C) sounds
    (D) scales

GO ON TO THE NEXT PAGE

5. A credit union can <u>distribute</u> earnings to its members as dividends.

   (A) increase
   (B) allocate
   (C) implement
   (D) augment

6. Silver was <u>eliminated from</u> quarters with the Coinage Act of 1965.

   (A) reduced from
   (B) added to
   (C) removed from
   (D) increased in

7. Plastics are synthetic resins that are made from such natural <u>sources</u> as coal, limestone, and petroleum.

   (A) organisms
   (B) materials
   (C) geological formations
   (D) origins

8. A catalytic converter in the exhaust system of a car will cause the carbon monoxide and hydrocarbons to convert to carbon dioxide and water <u>vapor</u>.

   (A) steam
   (B) liquid
   (C) resources
   (D) chemicals

9. There are <u>considerably</u> more weekly newspapers than daily newspapers in the United States.

   (A) mostly
   (B) hardly
   (C) rarely
   (D) substantially

10. It is possible for a chemist to use the melting point of a particular <u>substance</u> to determine its purity.

    (A) liquid
    (B) element
    (C) quantity
    (D) mixture

11. The <u>current</u> nickel, with a profile of Thomas Jefferson on the front and a picture of Monticello on the back, has been minted since 1938.

    (A) flowing
    (B) former
    (C) present
    (D) mixed

12. The purpose of the conference is to <u>address</u> the major issues that have been plaguing the constituency.

    (A) locate
    (B) augment
    (C) deal with
    (D) confiscate

13. The cacao tree, from whose seeds chocolate is made, flourishes in hot and <u>humid</u> climates.

    (A) temperate
    (B) damp
    (C) horrid
    (D) dry

14. Computerized editing systems are the <u>norm</u> in major newsrooms today.

    (A) rule
    (B) requirement
    (C) value
    (D) specialty

15. In the southeastern United States, freshwater bass may <u>grow</u> to 22 pounds.

    (A) farm
    (B) develop
    (C) exacerbate
    (D) accelerate

PRACTICE TEST FOUR

GO ON TO THE NEXT PAGE

16. The desert areas of the Southwest are <u>sparsely</u> inhabited.

    (A) heavily
    (B) merely
    (C) lightly
    (D) densely

17. In the United States 60 percent of the milk is <u>processed</u> into butter, cheese, ice cream, and other dairy products.

    (A) divided
    (B) separated
    (C) mixed
    (D) converted

18. Quinine has been used by doctors <u>chiefly</u> to treat malaria.

    (A) importantly
    (B) similarly
    (C) principally
    (D) momentarily

19. Mammoth Cave, in central Kentucky, contains several <u>subterranean</u> lakes, rivers, and waterfalls.

    (A) underground
    (B) large
    (C) deep
    (D) freshwater

20. One of the most common uses of boric acid is as <u>an antiseptic</u>.

    (A) a solvent
    (B) a bacteria
    (C) a compound
    (D) a disinfectant

21. The librarian <u>noted</u> that the book bindings were <u>damaged</u> during the photocopying process.

    (A) shouted
    (B) replied
    (C) complained
    (D) observed

22. Economists do not universally accept the <u>relevance</u> of diseconomies of scale.

    (A) expectation
    (B) pertinence
    (C) relationship
    (D) illustration

23. A female mosquito produces between 100 and 300 eggs <u>at a time</u> and up to 3,000 eggs during her lifetime.

    (A) at once
    (B) one by one
    (C) once in a while
    (D) off and on

24. Midway Island was <u>annexed</u> by the United States in 1859.

    (A) suppressed
    (B) acquired
    (C) coveted
    (D) obliterated

25. A raccoon is <u>distinctively</u> marked with a mask of black hair around its eyes.

    (A) uniquely
    (B) massively
    (C) primarily
    (D) defensively

26. A metal object such as a nail becomes a temporary magnet when it is within the <u>range</u> of a permanent magnet.

    (A) perspective
    (B) plane
    (C) field
    (D) variety

27. In colonial times in early America, a popular type of <u>social</u> gathering was the quilting bee.

    (A) political
    (B) communal
    (C) laborious
    (D) fastidious

GO ON TO THE NEXT PAGE

28. Since 1958 the United States has been attempting to achieve worldwide <u>unanimity</u> on control of pollution of the oceans.

    (A) animosity
    (B) involvement
    (C) agreement
    (D) interest

29. Walter Reed, a U.S. Army medical officer in Cuba in 1900, <u>daringly</u> conducted experiments to determine how yellow fever was transmitted.

    (A) scientifically
    (B) methodically
    (C) knowingly
    (D) courageously

30. Mammals have highly <u>developed</u> ears, consisting of varying <u>lengths</u> and numbers of turns in the cochlea.

    (A) sophisticated
    (B) aged
    (C) sensitized
    (D) acoustic

<u>Directions:</u> In the rest of this section you will read several passages. Each one is followed by several questions about it. For questions 31–60, you are to choose the <u>one</u> best answer, (A), (B), (C), or (D), to each question. Then, on your answer sheet, find <u>the</u> number of the question and fill in the space that corresponds to the letter of the answer you have chosen.

Answer all questions following a passage on the basis of what is <u>stated</u> or <u>implied</u> in that passage.

Read the following passage:

> John Quincy Adams, who served as the sixth president of the United States from 1825 to 1829, is today recognized for his masterful statesmanship and diplomacy. He dedicated his life to public service, both in the presidency and in the various other political offices he held. Throughout his political career he demonstrated his unswerving belief in freedom of speech, the anti-slavery cause, and the right of Americans to be free from European and Asian domination.

Example I

To what did John Quincy Adams devote his life?

(A) Improving his personal life
(B) Serving the public
(C) Increasing his fortune
(D) Working on his private business

Sample Answer

Ⓐ

ⓒ
Ⓓ

According to the passage, John Quincy Adams "dedicated his life to public service." Therefore, you should choose answer (B).

PRACTICE TEST FOUR

Example II

Sample Answer

The passage implies that John Quincy Adams held

Ⓐ
Ⓑ
Ⓒ
●

(A) no political offices
(B) only one political office
(C) exactly two political offices
(D) at least three political offices

The passage states that John Quincy Adams served in "the presidency and various other political offices." Therefore, you should choose answer (D).

After you read the directions, begin work on the questions.

GO ON TO THE NEXT PAGE ▶

Questions 31–35

Popular architecture in the United States in the beginning of the twentieth century paid respect to elaborately ornate historical motifs. The new skyscrapers sprouting up at the time were often ornately finished with elements of Gothic or Roman detailing.

During this period of emphasis on intricate ornamentation, certain architects began moving in a different direction, from the historic attention to ornate detailing toward more modern design typified by simplified flowing lines. Frank Lloyd Wright, the best-known of these early modern architects, started work in Chicago designing "prairie houses," long low buildings featuring flowing horizontal lines and simplistic unity of design. These buildings were intended to fit the wide open expanses of Midwest plains that served as a setting for Chicago. These "prairie houses," found in Chicago's suburban areas, served to tie the rapidly developing neighborhoods of Chicago with its plains heritage.

31. What is the main idea of this passage?

(A) The architectural style of Frank Lloyd Wright represented a change from earlier styles.
(B) Architecture in the twentieth century was very ornate.
(C) Frank Lloyd Wright's architecture was more elaborate than previous styles.
(D) Frank Lloyd Wright's "prairie houses" were well-known in Chicago.

32. According to the passage, the new skyscrapers built at the beginning of the twentieth century were

(A) elementary
(B) elaborately ornamented
(C) in a very modern style
(D) completely Gothic

33. Which of the following statements about Frank Lloyd Wright is supported in the passage?

(A) He was extremely popular prior to the twentieth century.
(B) He used elements of Gothic and Roman detailing in his work.
(C) His architectural style can be seen in Chicago's skyscrapers.
(D) His "prairie houses" were very different from the elaborately ornamented skyscrapers.

34. The "prairie houses" built by Frank Lloyd Wright were

(A) ornately detailed
(B) built in the Roman style
(C) skyscrapers
(D) long, flowing, and simple

35. According to the passage, how do Frank Lloyd Wright's "prairie houses" resemble the prairies around Chicago?

(A) They were covered with grass.
(B) They were rapidly developing.
(C) They were long and low.
(D) They were in Chicago.

GO ON TO THE NEXT PAGE

Questions 36–42

In the American colonies there was little money. England did not supply the colonies with coins and it did not allow the colonies to make their own coins, except for the Massachusetts Bay Colony, which received permission for a short period in 1652 to make several kinds of silver coins. England wanted to keep money out of America as a means of controlling trade: America was forced to trade only with England if it did not have the money to buy products from other countries. The result during this pre-revolutionary period was that the colonists used various goods in place of money: beaver pelts, Indian wampum, and tobacco leaves were all commonly used substitutes for money. The colonists also made use of any foreign coins they could obtain. Dutch, Spanish, French, and English coins were all in use in the American colonies.

During the Revolutionary War, funds were needed to finance the war, so each of the individual states and the Continental Congress issued paper money. So much of this paper money was printed that by the end of the war it was virtually worthless. As a result, trade in goods and the use of foreign coins still flourished during this period.

By the time the Revolutionary War had been won by the American colonists, the monetary system was in a state of total disarray. To remedy this situation, the new Constitution of the United States, approved in 1789, allowed only Congress to issue money. The individual states could no longer have their own money supply. A few years later, the Coinage Act of 1792 made the dollar the official currency of the United States and put the country on a bimetallic standard. In this bimetallic system, both gold and silver were legal money, and the rate of exchange of silver to gold was fixed by the government at sixteen to one.

36. This passage mainly discusses

(A) American money from past to present
(B) the English monetary policies in colonial America
(C) the effect of the Revolution on American money
(D) the American monetary system of the seventeenth and eighteenth centuries

37. The passage indicates that during the colonial period, money was

(A) supplied by England
(B) coined freely by the colonists
(C) scarce
(D) used extensively for trade

38. The Massachusetts Bay Colony was allowed to make coins

(A) continuously from the inception of the colony
(B) throughout the seventeenth century
(C) from 1652 until the Revolutionary War
(D) for a short time during one year

39. Which of the following is NOT mentioned in the passage as a substitute for money during the colonial period?

(A) Wampum
(B) Cotton
(C) Tobacco
(D) Beaver furs

GO ON TO THE NEXT PAGE

40. According to the passage, what happened to the American monetary system during the Revolutionary War?

    (A) The Continental Congress issued gold and silver coins.
    (B) Individual states were not allowed to issue money.
    (C) So much paper money was circulated that it lost its value.
    (D) American money replaced trade in goods and foreign coins.

41. How was the monetary system arranged in the Constitution?

    (A) Only the U.S. Congress could issue money.
    (B) The U.S. officially went on a bimetallic monetary system.
    (C) Various state governments, including Massachusetts, could issue money.
    (D) The dollar was made the official currency of the U.S.

42. According to the passage, which of the following is NOT true about the bimetallic monetary system?

    (A) Either gold or silver could be used as official money.
    (B) Gold could be exchanged for silver at a rate of 16 to 1.
    (C) The monetary system was based on two metals.
    (D) It was established in 1792.

GO ON TO THE NEXT PAGE

Questions 43–47

Louisa May Alcott, an American author best known for her children's books *Little Women*, *Little Men*, and *Jo's Boys*, was profoundly influenced by her family, particularly her father. She was the daughter of Bronson Alcott, a well-known teacher, intellectual, and free thinker who advocated abolitionism, women's rights, and vegetarianism long before they were popular. He was called a man of unparalleled intellect by his friend Ralph Waldo Emerson. Bronson Alcott instilled in his daughter his lofty and spiritual values and in return was idolized by his daughter. Louisa used her father as a model for the impractical yet serenely wise and adored father in *Little Women*, and with the success of this novel she was able to provide for her family, giving her father the financial security that until then he had never experienced.

43. This passage mainly discusses

  (A) Louisa May Alcott's famous books
  (B) how Bronson Alcott implemented his educational philosophies
  (C) the success of *Little Women*
  (D) Bronson Alcott's influence on his daughter

44. The passage implies that vegetarianism

  (A) was more popular than abolitionism
  (B) was the reason for Louisa's adoration for her father
  (C) became popular in a later period
  (D) was one of the reasons for Bronson Alcott's unparalleled intellect

45. In line 6, the word "lofty" is closest in meaning to

  (A) commonplace
  (B) high-minded
  (C) self-serving
  (D) sympathetic

46. It can be inferred from the passage that Louisa May Alcott used the success of *Little Women* to

  (A) buy herself anything she had ever wanted
  (B) achieve personal financial security
  (C) give her father tangible proof of her love
  (D) detach herself from her family

47. The author's purpose in the passage is to

  (A) explain how an author becomes famous
  (B) describe the influence of family on a writer
  (C) support Bronson Alcott's educational theories
  (D) show the success that can be achieved by an author

GO ON TO THE NEXT PAGE

Questions 48–54

The brain of the average human weighs approximately 14 kilograms and consists of three main parts—the cerebrum, the cerebellum, and the brain stem. The cerebrum is by far the largest of the three parts, taking up 85% of the brain by weight. The outside layer of the cerebrum, the cerebral cortex, is a grooved and bumpy surface covering the nerve cells beneath. The various sections of the cerebrum are the sensory cortex, which is responsible for receiving and decoding sensory messages from throughout the body; the motor cortex, which sends action instructions to the skeletal muscles; and the association cortex, which receives, monitors, and processes information. It is in the association cortex that the processes that allow humans to think take place. The cerebellum, located below the cerebrum in the back part of the skull, is the section of the brain that controls balance and posture. The brain stem connects the cerebrum and the spinal cord. It controls various body processes such as breathing and heartbeat.

48. What is the author's main purpose?

(A) To describe the functions of the parts of the brain
(B) To explain how the brain processes information
(C) To demonstrate the physical composition of the brain
(D) To give examples of human body functions

49. The passage states that the most massive part of the brain is the

(A) cerebrum
(B) cerebellum
(C) cerebral cortex
(D) brain stem

50. How does the passage describe the appearance of the cerebral cortex?

(A) As smooth
(B) As 85% of the brain by weight
(C) As a layer of the cerebellum
(D) As ridged

51. According to the passage, which part of the brain analyzes information?

(A) The sensory cortex
(B) The association cortex
(C) The cerebellum
(D) The brain stem

52. The sensory cortex

(A) senses that messages should be sent out to the muscles.
(B) provides a surface covering for nerve cells.
(C) is where the human process of thinking occurs.
(D) receives and processes information from the senses.

53. Which of the following is true about the cerebellum?

(A) It is located above the cerebrum.
(B) It controls breathing.
(C) It is responsible for balance.
(D) It is the outside layer of the cerebrum.

54. What shape does the brain stem most likely have?

(A) Small and round
(B) Long and thin
(C) Large and formless
(D) Short and flat

GO ON TO THE NEXT PAGE

Questions 55–60

In west-central New York State there is a group of eleven long, narrow lakes known as the Finger Lakes. These lakes have been aptly named because of their resemblance to the fingers of a hand. Two of the largest of the Finger Lakes, Seneca and Cayuga, exemplify the selection of the name: Seneca is 37 miles long and 4 miles across at its widest point, and Cayuga is 40 miles long and 2 miles across. Although scientists are uncertain as to how these lakes were formed, most believe that glacial ice forged out the valleys to a depth well below sea level, and with the melting of the glaciers the lakes were formed.

55. How could the Finger Lakes be described?

   (A) As basically circular
   (B) As all the same size
   (C) As tiny
   (D) As long and thin

56. According to the passage, why are these lakes known as Finger Lakes?

   (A) They are the same size as fingers.
   (B) Their shape is similar to a finger's.
   (C) Their composition is the same as a finger's.
   (D) There are as many lakes as there are fingers.

57. Why does the author mention Seneca and Cayuga Lakes?

   (A) They are the only two Finger Lakes.
   (B) They are the two largest lakes in the United States.
   (C) They are good examples of long and narrow Finger Lakes.
   (D) They are long and wide.

58. The passage implies that Seneca Lake is

   (A) a constant 4 miles wide
   (B) at least 4 miles wide at each point
   (C) wider than it is long
   (D) narrower than 4 miles at certain points

59. What do most scientists believe caused the formation of the Finger Lakes?

   (A) The sea level decreased.
   (B) Heavy rainfalls flooded the area.
   (C) The melted glaciers carved out the valleys.
   (D) Glaciers cut into the land and then melted to fill the valleys.

60. What is the tone of this passage?

   (A) Informative
   (B) Accusatory
   (C) Humorous
   (D) Calculating

THIS IS THE END OF SECTION 3

IF YOU FINISH BEFORE TIME IS CALLED, CHECK YOUR WORK
ON SECTION 3 ONLY.
DO NOT READ OR WORK ON ANY OTHER SECTION OF THE TEST.

TEST OF WRITTEN ENGLISH: ESSAY QUESTION

Time—30 minutes

Study the graphs describing three possible plans for the use of programming time at a public service television station. Then respond to the question.

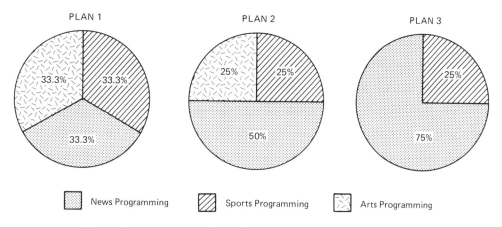

Three Programming Plans for a Public Service TV Station

You are the programming director for a public service television station. The station is considering three different plans for dividing its programming time. Select the plan that you believe would best serve the public. Then justify your choice.

Write your answer on the answer sheet for the Test of Written English, Practice Test Four, on pages 181–182.

SECTION 1
LISTENING COMPREHENSION

In this section of the test, you will have an opportunity to demonstrate your ability to understand spoken English. There are three parts in this section, with special directions for each part.

Part A

Directions: For each question in Part A, you will hear a short sentence. Each sentence will be spoken just one time. The sentences you hear will not be written out for you. Therefore, you must listen carefully to understand what the speaker says.

After you hear a sentence, read the four choices in your test book, marked (A), (B), (C), and (D), and decide which one is closest in meaning to the sentence you heard. Then, on your answer sheet, find the number of the question and fill in the space that corresponds to the letter of the answer you have chosen. Fill in the space so the letter inside the oval cannot be seen.

Example I   Sample Answer

You will hear: ● Ⓑ Ⓒ Ⓓ

You will read: (A) John outran the others.
                (B) John was the fastest hunter
                        in the chase.
                (C) John wasn't the slowest in the race.
                (D) John was the last runner to
                        finish the race.

The speaker said, "John was the fastest runner in the race." Sentence (A), "John outran the others," is closest in meaning to the sentence you heard. Therefore, you should choose answer (A).

Example II   Sample Answer

You will hear: Ⓐ Ⓑ ● Ⓓ

You will read: (A) Could you help me use the rest?
                (B) Do you mind using the other
                        desk?
                (C) Would you mind helping me
                        carry this piece of furniture?
                (D) If you move my desk, I'll help
                        you with your work.

The speaker said, "Could you help me move my desk?" Sentence (C), "Would you mind helping me carry this piece of furniture?" is closest in meaning to the sentence you heard. Therefore, you should choose answer (C).

114   PRACTICE TEST FIVE

1. (A) Both Alice and Joe finished journalism school.
   (B) Alice and Joe gradually talked to the journalist.
   (C) Before school, Alice and Joe wrote in their journals.
   (D) The graduation ceremony for Alice and Joe was observed by journalists.

2. (A) I'll be very careful with Bill.
   (B) I'll watch Bill.
   (C) I'll pay the money.
   (D) I'll be cautious with the money.

3. (A) It's fair for the university students to find their own apartments.
   (B) It's not too difficult to find housing near campus.
   (C) It's easy to find students in their apartments.
   (D) It's quite difficult to locate apartments near the university.

4. (A) Was the seminar ongoing?
   (B) Wasn't the summer quiet and boring?
   (C) The seminar wasn't quiet, was it?
   (D) Did you think the discussion was boring, too?

5. (A) Tonight you need to load your truck.
   (B) Your lawn should be watered tonight.
   (C) You should keep your lawn dry.
   (D) You must wash your clothes this evening.

6. (A) Would you like to go for a stroll by the ocean?
   (B) Do you want to wait for the speech after dinner?
   (C) Shall we walk to the beach to have dinner?
   (D) Should we rest after dinner or go to the beach?

7. (A) It couldn't be too hot to work.
   (B) I didn't accomplish much because of the weather.
   (C) I completed a lot of work in spite of the hot weather.
   (D) Unless it's very hot, I don't get much work done.

8. (A) The president of the student council voted for him.
   (B) He counseled students about the election.
   (C) The students selected him to be council president.
   (D) He helped to elect the president of the student council.

9. (A) It's important to issue the right car keys.
   (B) The issue's about the importance of having a car.
   (C) Car insurance is essential.
   (D) Take care when you discuss the importance of the issue.

10. (A) Were you ready to leave on time?
    (B) When will you have read it?
    (C) How long have you been waiting?
    (D) What time can we go?

11. (A) Adam's younger than his brother and sister.
    (B) Adam's brother is younger than his sister.
    (C) Adam's the oldest of three children.
    (D) Adam's brothers and sisters are all younger than Adam.

12. (A) This is the second largest football crowd ever.
    (B) This is the only time that a large crowd has attended a football game.
    (C) The large crowd has attended only one football game.
    (D) The football game was played in front of a large crowd only once.

PRACTICE TEST FIVE

GO ON TO THE NEXT PAGE

13. (A) Steve heard a noise while studying for economics.
    (B) Steve's grade in economics was not too bad.
    (C) Steve's economics grade upset him.
    (D) Steve's annoyed about the graduate degree in economics.

14. (A) The two classes meet in an hour and a half.
    (B) This class meets three hours per week.
    (C) Each half of the class is an hour long.
    (D) Two times a week the class meets for an hour.

15. (A) I hope to find you here when I return.
    (B) I won't accept your findings when I'm back.
    (C) You shouldn't expect for me to return.
    (D) I was surprised that you were still here.

16. (A) The boys screamed while they played.
    (B) The boys' screams could be heard all over the football field.
    (C) The football players put some ice on their sore muscles.
    (D) First the boys played, and then they had a snack.

17. (A) Maybe you can leave on the next plane.
    (B) I hope that your next fight will be more successful.
    (C) Hopefully you can get on with your life.
    (D) I believe in your ability to get over the fight.

18. (A) You need to write questions better.
    (B) You certainly must make your writing better.
    (C) Without the questions, you cannot write the answers.
    (D) You need to understand the written questions better.

19. (A) Because of all her reviews, she's quite famous.
    (B) She wasn't the most famous person seen at the reception.
    (C) Critics think her work's good, but she's not well-known by the public.
    (D) Because of the fame of the reviewer, she was well received.

20. (A) I probably left the office with the file.
    (B) The file of letters must be to the left of my desk in my office.
    (C) The file folder must be in my office.
    (D) I must have left my office to file the letters.

Part B

Directions: In Part B you will hear short conversations between two speakers. At the end of each conversation, a third person will ask a question about what was said. You will hear each conversation and question about it just one time. Therefore, you must listen carefully to understand what each speaker says. After you hear a conversation and the question about it, read the four possible answers in your test book and decide which one is the best answer to the question you heard. Then, on your answer sheet, find the number of the question and fill in the space that corresponds to the letter of the answer you have chosen.

GO ON TO THE NEXT PAGE

Look at the following example.

You will hear:

You will read:
- (A) The exam was really awful.
- (B) It was the worst exam she had ever seen.
- (C) It couldn't have been more difficult.
- (D) It wasn't that hard.

From the conversation you learn that the man thought the exam was very difficult and that the woman disagreed with the man. The best answer to the question "What does the woman mean?" is (D), "It wasn't that hard." Therefore, you should choose answer (D).

21.
- (A) He doubts the weather will be bad.
- (B) He probably won't go skiing.
- (C) He thinks the weather won't be as bad as predicted.
- (D) The weather forecaster didn't do a good job.

22.
- (A) She only spent a few cents.
- (B) She couldn't find a lot of money in her purse.
- (C) She spent all she had.
- (D) It wasn't fair to spend the money in her purse.

23.
- (A) A library.
- (B) A bookstore.
- (C) A classroom.
- (D) A newspaper office.

24.
- (A) That she should sit down in psychology class.
- (B) That she should go to class before trying to read the chapter.
- (C) That he should provide a chapter to read.
- (D) That she should prepare for class.

25.
- (A) He should find some new clothes.
- (B) He should have his clothes cleaned in a different place.
- (C) He should look for a way to do his own laundry.
- (D) He should give the laundry another chance.

26.
- (A) She knows he's not seriously injured.
- (B) She hopes he'll get to the hospital quickly.
- (C) She's heard all about his illness.
- (D) She doesn't know how he's doing.

27.
- (A) It's time to go home.
- (B) He's late for an appointment.
- (C) His home's far away.
- (D) He's ready to leave home.

28.
- (A) He doesn't think it's enough medicine.
- (B) Taking pills every day should help her a lot.
- (C) It seems like too much medicine.
- (D) Maybe there aren't enough pills.

GO ON TO THE NEXT PAGE

29. (A) She was unaware of the
        tornado.
    (B) A tornado came dangerously
        close to her.
    (C) The tornado came in through
        the window.
    (D) She climbed out of the window
        when the tornado came.

30. (A) That the sweater's too warm.
    (B) That the weather in Hawaii is
        hot.
    (C) That the woman will get cold on
        vacation.
    (D) That the woman hasn't packed
        for the trip.

31. (A) He must study about turtles for
        his exam.
    (B) He comprehends that he must
        prepare for his exams.
    (C) He'll prepare for his exams
        after he moves.
    (D) He's not accomplishing very
        much.

32. (A) The printer was supposed to
        arrive weeks ago.
    (B) Everyone's talking excitedly
        about the new printer.
    (C) The new printer should arrive in
        a few weeks.
    (D) The computer lab is four weeks
        old now.

33. (A) He needs to talk to her
        immediately.
    (B) It bothers him to talk with her.
    (C) Tomorrow is too late for their
        discussion.
    (D) He doesn't have anything very
        important to say.

34. (A) This report is better than the last.
    (B) It's better to publish the report
        annually.
    (C) He feels better about the report.
    (D) The report isn't too good.

35. (A) He's unable to go to the opera.
    (B) He isn't very fond of opera.
    (C) He likes going to the opera
        occasionally.
    (D) He has a dentist appointment
        tonight.

Part C

Directions: In this part of the test, you will hear short talks and conversations. After each of them, you will be asked some questions. You will hear the talks and conversations and the questions about them just one time. They will not be written out for you. Therefore, you must listen carefully to understand what each speaker says.

After you hear a question, read the four possible answers in your test book and decide which one is the best answer to the question you heard. Then, on your answer sheet, find the number of the question and fill in the space that corresponds to the letter of the answer you have chosen.

Listen to this sample talk.

You will hear:

Now look at the following example.

GO ON TO THE NEXT PAGE ➤

You will hear: Sample Answer

You will read: (A) Art from America's inner cities.   Ⓐ Ⓑ Ⓒ ●
                (B) Art from the central region
                     of the U.S.
                (C) Art from various urban areas
                     in the U.S.
                (D) Art from rural sections of
                     America.

The best answer to the question "What style of painting is known as American regionalist?" is (D), "Art from rural sections of America." Therefore, you should choose answer (D).

Now look at the next example.

You will hear: Sample Answer

You will read: (A) *American Regionalist.*   Ⓐ Ⓑ ● Ⓓ
                (B) *The Family Farm in Iowa.*
                (C) *American Gothic.*
                (D) *A Serious Couple.*

The best answer to the question "What is the name of Wood's most successful painting?" is (C), "*American Gothic.*" Therefore, you should choose answer (C).

36. (A) A university administrator.
    (B) A fellow student.
    (C) A librarian.
    (D) A registrar.

37. (A) How to use the library.
    (B) The university registration
         procedure.
    (C) Services offered by the Student
         Center.
    (D) Important locations on campus.

38. (A) It isn't open many hours.
    (B) It's where students buy texts for
         their courses.
    (C) It's large and has a complete
         range of materials.
    (D) It's often used for registration.

39. (A) To provide students with
         assistance and amusement.
    (B) To assist students in the
         registration process.
    (C) To allow students to watch
         movies.
    (D) To provide textbooks for
         university courses.

40. (A) In administrators' offices.
    (B) In the Student Center.
    (C) In an auditorium.
    (D) In the Student Records office.

41. (A) To a doctor's appointment.
    (B) To an exercise club.
    (C) To a swimming pool.
    (D) To a school.

GO ON TO THE NEXT PAGE ➤

PRACTICE TEST FIVE   **119**

42. (A) They're both regular members.
    (B) He likes to go there occasionally.
    (C) She wants him to try it out.
    (D) She hates to exercise alone.

43. (A) He doesn't like to exercise.
    (B) The health club's too popular.
    (C) Perhaps he prefers other kinds of exercise.
    (D) Only members are allowed.

44. (A) A limited number.
    (B) Racketball courts and a swimming pool.
    (C) Exercise machines, but not classes.
    (D) Just about anything.

45. (A) Visit the club once.
    (B) Take out a membership.
    (C) Try the club unless he hurts himself.
    (D) See if he has time to go.

46. (A) Natural soaps.
    (B) Synthetic detergents.
    (C) Biodegradable detergents.
    (D) Phosphates.

47. (A) Synthetic detergents.
    (B) A major cause of water pollution.
    (C) Substances that break down into simpler forms.
    (D) The reason for the foaming water supply.

48. (A) They broke down into simpler forms.
    (B) They caused the water to become foamy.
    (C) They released phosphates into the water.
    (D) They damaged only the underground water supply.

49. (A) Non-biodegradable synthetic detergents were introduced.
    (B) The new detergents caused foamy water.
    (C) The new detergents wouldn't break down into simpler forms.
    (D) The new biodegradable detergents contained phosphates.

50. (A) Water pollution in the 1950's.
    (B) Non-biodegradable synthetic detergents.
    (C) The foamy water supply.
    (D) Problems caused by phosphates.

THIS IS THE END OF THE LISTENING COMPREHENSION SECTION OF THE TEST

THE NEXT PART OF THE TEST IS SECTION 2. TURN TO THE
DIRECTIONS FOR SECTION 2 IN YOUR TEST BOOK.
READ THEM, AND BEGIN WORK.
DO NOT READ OR WORK ON ANY OTHER SECTION OF THE TEST.

SECTION 2
STRUCTURE AND WRITTEN EXPRESSION
Time—25 minutes

This section is designed to measure your ability to recognize language that is appropriate for standard written English. There are two types of questions in this section, with special directions for each type.

Directions: Questions 1–15 are incomplete sentences. Beneath each sentence you will see four words or phrases, marked (A), (B), (C), and (D). Choose the one word or phrase that best completes the sentence. Then, on your answer sheet, find the number of the question and fill in the space that corresponds to the letter of the answer you have chosen. Fill in the space so that the letter inside the oval cannot be seen.

Example I   Sample Answer

The president _____ the election   ● Ⓑ Ⓒ Ⓓ
by a landslide.

(A) won
(B) he won
(C) yesterday
(D) fortunately

The sentence should read, "The president won the election by a landslide." Therefore, you should choose answer (A).

Example II   Sample Answer

When _____ the conference?   Ⓐ ● Ⓒ Ⓓ

(A) the doctor attended
(B) did the doctor attend
(C) the doctor will attend
(D) the doctor's attendance

The sentence should read, "When did the doctor attend the conference?" Therefore, you should choose answer (B).

After you read the directions, begin work on the questions.

1. Jackson, Mississippi, _____ capital, is the largest city in the state.

    (A) the
    (B) where is the
    (C) is the
    (D) it is the

2. It is the recommendation of the U.S. Public Health Service _____ all children be vaccinated against a variety of diseases.

    (A) for
    (B) that
    (C) when
    (D) suggests

PRACTICE TEST FIVE

GO ON TO THE NEXT PAGE

3. In 1774 delegates from all colonies _____ attended the First Continental Congress.

   (A) Georgia
   (B) the exception was Georgia
   (C) except Georgia
   (D) except that Georgia was

4. Valley Forge National Park commemorates the time that Washington _____ in Valley Forge with his troops.

   (A) spend
   (B) spent
   (C) was spent
   (D) has been spent

5. In New England _____ picturesque fishing villages and manufacturing towns.

   (A) has
   (B) many
   (C) about
   (D) there are

6. The pirate Jean Lafitte offered his services to the U.S. government in the War of 1812, _____ in 1815, and received a full pardon from President James Madison.

   (A) fought in the Battle of New Orleans
   (B) the Battle of New Orleans was
   (C) he fought in the Battle of New Orleans
   (D) the Battle of New Orleans

7. Although fish do not have any outer ears, _____ have a simple inner ear on either side of the head.

   (A) there are varieties
   (B) they are varieties
   (C) some varieties
   (D) which varieties

8. Jamestown, the first permanent English settlement in America, _____ in 1607.

   (A) it was founded
   (B) colonists arrived
   (C) was established
   (D) founded

9. Before _____ Stephen A. Douglas took part in a series of debates with Lincoln on the slavery issue.

   (A) the Civil War
   (B) the Civil War was
   (C) the Civil War with
   (D) it happened that the Civil War

10. _____ through a telescope, Venus appears to go through changes in size and shape.

    (A) It is seen
    (B) Seeing
    (C) When seen
    (D) It has seen

11. The various types of bacteria are classified according to _____ shaped.

    (A) they have
    (B) having
    (C) how they are
    (D) whose

12. Beavers have been known to use logs, branches, rocks, and mud to build dams that are more than a thousand _____.

    (A) foot in length
    (B) feet long
    (C) long feet
    (D) lengthy foot

GO ON TO THE NEXT PAGE

13. _____ as the most important crop in Hawaii is sugar cane.

    (A) It ranks
    (B) It is ranked
    (C) What ranks
    (D) The rank

14. _____ stone tools and animal remains found with the human fossils, anthropologists have determined that Neanderthal Man was a successful hunter.

    (A) When the
    (B) The
    (C) Both the
    (D) From the

15. In the U.S. more than 60 percent of all high school students who _____ continue their education.

    (A) do not
    (B) graduate
    (C) will
    (D) can

Directions: In questions 16–40 each sentence has four underlined words or phrases. The four underlined parts of the sentence are marked (A), (B), (C), and (D). Identify the one underlined word or phrase that must be changed in order for the sentence to be correct. Then, on your answer sheet, find the number of the question and fill in the space that corresponds to the letter of the answer you have chosen.

Example I   Sample Answer

The four string on a violin are tuned in fifths.   Ⓐ ● Ⓒ Ⓓ
  A   B   C D

The sentence should read, "The four strings on a violin are tuned in fifths." Therefore, you should choose answer (B).

Example II   Sample Answer

The research for the book *Roots* taking Alex Haley   Ⓐ Ⓑ ● Ⓓ
     A   B   C
twelve years.
    D

The sentence should read, "The research for the book *Roots* took Alex Haley twelve years." Therefore, you should choose answer (C).

After you read the directions, begin work on the questions.

PRACTICE TEST FIVE   GO ON TO THE NEXT PAGE ▶

16. <u>Together</u> Rogers and Hammerstein wrote nine <u>musicals</u>, the <u>first</u> of <u>whose</u> was
       A   B   C   D

    Oklahoma (1943).

17. J. Edgar Hoover <u>has served</u> as <u>director</u> of the FBI <u>from</u> 1924 until <u>his death</u> in 1972.
                     A   B   C   D

18. <u>For photosynthesis</u> <u>to occur</u>, a leaf <u>requires</u> carbon dioxide, water, and
          A   B   C

    <u>light is also necessary</u>.
          D

19. Denver is <u>call</u> the "Mile High City" because <u>it is</u> at <u>an altitude</u> of 5,280 <u>feet</u>, or one
            A   B   C   D

    mile, above sea level.

20. A neutrino is <u>a subatomic</u> particle <u>it</u> <u>has</u> <u>no</u> electrical charge.
                   A   B C D

21. <u>While</u> the sun is <u>the major</u> source of ultraviolet rays, <u>it is</u> not the <u>source only</u>.
      A   B   C   D

22. Gamma globulin, a protein <u>found in</u> blood plasma, <u>it is</u> used to prevent <u>such</u>
                           A   B   C

    infectious diseases <u>as</u> measles and viral hepatitis.
                    D

23. Nuclear <u>powers</u> production in the U.S. <u>is</u> <u>controlled</u> by <u>the</u> Nuclear Regulatory
             A   B   C   D

    Commission (NRC).

24. A dam <u>stops</u> the flow <u>of water</u>, creating <u>a</u> reservoir and <u>raise</u> the level of water.
         A   B   C   D

25. After <u>learned</u> to print, <u>elementary</u> school <u>children</u> learn cursive <u>writing</u>.
        A   B   C   D

26. <u>Authors</u> Samuel Eliot Morison <u>won</u> two Pultizer Prizes, one in 1943 for <u>a biography</u>
      A   B   C

    of Columbus and <u>the other</u> in 1960 for a biography of John Paul Jones.
                    D

27. The United States is the <u>world's</u> largest cheese producer, <u>making</u> more than two
                        A   B

    million <u>tons</u> of cheese <u>annual</u>.
          C   D

GO ON TO THE NEXT PAGE

28. The system <u>for helping</u> slaves escape to the north was called the "Underground
             A

    Railroad," <u>though</u> <u>it</u> was neither underground <u>or</u> a railroad.
            B   C   D

29. Natural gas is <u>compose</u> of hydrocarbon molecules <u>that break</u> <u>apart into</u> hydrogen
               A   B   C

    and carbon atoms <u>when heated</u>.
                  D

30. Diamonds <u>are evaluated</u> on <u>the basis of</u> <u>their</u> <u>weigh</u>, purity, and color.
               A   B   C   D

31. <u>According the</u> kinetic theory, all matter <u>consists</u> of <u>constantly</u> <u>moving</u> particles.
        A   B   C   D

32. Harvard University <u>was</u> established <u>just</u> <u>after sixteen years</u> the Pilgrims <u>arrived</u>.
                  A   B   C   D

33. Patients <u>suffering</u> <u>from</u> encephalitis have an <u>inflammatory</u> of <u>the brain</u>.
            A   B   C   D

34. Although <u>it can</u> be <u>closely nearly</u> approached, absolute zero cannot <u>be reached</u>
              A   B   C

    <u>experimentally</u>.
       D

35. <u>Because</u> helicopters are capable <u>of hovering</u> in midair, they are <u>particularly</u> useful
      A   B   C

    for rescue missions, military <u>operates</u>, and transportation.
                               D

36. Many states <u>do</u> laws <u>regulating</u> <u>production processes</u> for different <u>types of</u> food
              A   B   C   D

    products.

37. According to the 1978 Bakke decision by the Supreme Court, <u>an</u> university may not
                                                    A

    <u>use</u> admissions <u>quotas</u> to obtain <u>a racially</u> balanced student body.
     B   C   D

38. Ester Forbes <u>won</u> the 1943 Pulitzer Prize <u>in</u> American history for <u>her</u> <u>biographer</u> of
                A   B   C   D

    Paul Revere.

39. The Bill of Rights <u>was added</u> to the Constitution <u>specifically</u> to guarantee certain
                      A   B

    <u>the</u> individual <u>rights</u>.
     C   D

PRACTICE TEST FIVE

GO ON TO THE NEXT PAGE ➤

40. <u>Unlike</u> light from other sources, <u>which</u> travels in all <u>direction</u>, the light from a
      ㅤㅤ A ㅤㅤㅤㅤㅤㅤㅤㅤㅤㅤㅤ B ㅤㅤㅤㅤㅤㅤㅤㅤ C

ㅤㅤlaser is <u>highly directional</u>.
ㅤㅤㅤㅤㅤㅤㅤ D

THIS IS THE END OF SECTION 2

IF YOU FINISH BEFORE TIME IS CALLED, CHECK YOUR WORK
ON SECTION 2 ONLY.
DO NOT READ OR WORK ON ANY OTHER SECTION OF THE TEST.
THE SUPERVISOR WILL TELL YOU WHEN TO BEGIN
WORK ON SECTION 3.

SECTION 3
VOCABULARY AND READING COMPREHENSION
Time—45 minutes

This section is designed to measure your comprehension of standard written English. There are two types of questions in this section, with special directions for each type.

Directions: In questions 1–30 each sentence has an underlined word or phrase. Below each sentence are four other words or phrases, marked (A), (B), (C), and (D). You are to choose the one word or phrase that best keeps the meaning of the original sentence if it is substituted for the underlined word or phrase. Then, on your answer sheet, find the number of the question and fill in the space that corresponds to the letter you have chosen. Fill in the space so that the letter inside the oval cannot be seen.

Example I   Sample Answer

   Both boats and trains are used
   for transporting the materials.

   (A) planes
   (B) ships
   (C) canoes
   (D) railroads

The best answer is (B) because "Both ships and trains are used for transporting the materials" is closest in meaning to the original sentence. Therefore, you should choose answer (B).

After you read the directions, begin work on the questions.

1. The average age of the inhabitants is 27.6 years.

   (A) remains
   (B) visitors
   (C) wayfarers
   (D) residents

2. Cambridge, Massachusetts, is sometimes called "University City" because of the famous schools located there.

   (A) built
   (B) begun
   (C) incited
   (D) situated

3. Because of an increase in mosquitoes and malaria, city officials have instituted an eradication program.

   (A) authorities
   (B) laborers
   (C) offices
   (D) builders

4. The change in population distribution was barely noticeable to the demographers conducting the study.

   (A) often
   (B) hardly
   (C) never
   (D) softly

5. The Baltimore oriole has wings with white bars and a <u>bright</u> orange breast.

   (A) light
   (B) brilliant
   (C) intelligent
   (D) illuminated

6. Of the approximately 400 billion <u>packages</u> used yearly in the United States, half are for food and drink.

   (A) posters
   (B) suitcases
   (C) dishes
   (D) containers

7. The colony of Pennsylvania was <u>founded</u> by William Penn, an English Quaker, in 1681.

   (A) established
   (B) recovered
   (C) located
   (D) governed

8. The world's <u>busiest</u> airport is Chicago's O'Hare, where each year 550,000 flights land and take off.

   (A) best run
   (B) most active
   (C) most spacious
   (D) most successful

9. Around 150 B.C. the Greek astronomer Hipparchus developed a system to <u>classify</u> stars according to brightness.

   (A) shine
   (B) record
   (C) categorize
   (D) diversify

10. More maple syrup is produced in the Canadian province of Quebec than is produced in the <u>entire</u> United States.

    (A) continental
    (B) whole
    (C) complex
    (D) extreme

11. Among other duties, the Federal Communications Commission is <u>charged with</u> the licensing of radio and television stations.

    (A) excited by
    (B) held responsible for
    (C) billed for
    (D) attacked by

12. In the 1980 census, New Jersey was the most <u>densely</u> populated state.

    (A) rigorously
    (B) heavily
    (C) wantonly
    (D) searingly

13. A word <u>formed from</u> the initials of a compound term is an acronym.

    (A) found in
    (B) shaped like
    (C) taken to
    (D) created from

14. Approximately one-fifth of the earth's land <u>surface</u> is composed of desert.

    (A) exterior
    (B) core
    (C) mass
    (D) bottom

15. In the 1776 pamphlet "Common Sense," Thomas Paine <u>defended</u> the cause of the American Revolution.

    (A) fought
    (B) championed
    (C) exposed
    (D) believed

GO ON TO THE NEXT PAGE

16. The General Motors Corporation is the <u>principal</u> industry in Pontiac, Michigan.

    (A) chief
    (B) oldest
    (C) earliest
    (D) automotive

17. The calf of the human leg <u>contains</u> seven muscles.

    (A) includes
    (B) requires
    (C) makes use of
    (D) depends on

18. The question of why prehistoric animals became extinct has not been <u>conclusively</u> answered.

    (A) predominantly
    (B) extensively
    (C) especially
    (D) decisively

19. Despite the breakthrough, expectations remain <u>modest.</u>

    (A) thorough
    (B) slight
    (C) intricate
    (D) shy

20. The Lincoln Tunnel <u>connects</u> midtown New York and Weehawken, New Jersey.

    (A) separates
    (B) substantiates
    (C) links
    (D) divides

21. The tetracyclines are a family of antibiotics used to fight <u>infection</u>.

    (A) battles
    (B) contamination
    (C) injury
    (D) deterioration

22. Francis Marion became known as the "Swamp Fox" during the American Revolution because he and his soldiers <u>successfully</u> used the South Carolina swamps as a base camp for raids on the British.

    (A) effectively
    (B) cunningly
    (C) treacherously
    (D) actively

23. James K. Polk was president of the United States from 1845 to 1849, a period of tremendous territorial <u>expansion</u>.

    (A) inclusion
    (B) expression
    (C) detraction
    (D) growth

24. Macrame is used to make clothing and accessories as well as <u>ornamental</u> items.

    (A) colorful
    (B) decorative
    (C) utilitarian
    (D) hand-made

25. Pain signals, in the form of electrical <u>impulses,</u> are carried to the brain by the nerves.

    (A) hurts
    (B) lights
    (C) cells
    (D) shocks

26. The planet Pluto travels around the sun in <u>an elliptical</u> orbit approximately once every 248 years.

    (A) an oval
    (B) a slow
    (C) a tremendous
    (D) an unchanging

GO ON TO THE NEXT PAGE

27. The midnight sun is caused when the earth <u>tilts</u> toward the sun.

    (A) folds
    (B) bends
    (C) inclines
    (D) rotates

28. The biography is a very popular form of <u>prose</u>.

    (A) life story
    (B) poetry
    (C) historical work
    (D) writing

29. Midshipmen have <u>drilled</u> at the United States Naval Academy at Annapolis since 1845.

    (A) studied
    (B) trained
    (C) sailed
    (D) worked

30. In the Petrified Forest National Park, huge chunks of fossilized wood are surrounded by <u>numerous</u> smaller fragments.

    (A) varied
    (B) numbered
    (C) counted
    (D) myriad

<u>Directions</u>: In the rest of this section you will read several passages. Each one is followed by several questions about it. For questions 31–60, you are to choose the <u>one</u> best answer, (A), (B), (C), or (D), to each question. Then, on your answer sheet, find the number of the question and fill in the space that corresponds to the letter of the answer you have chosen.

Answer all questions following a passage on the basis of what is <u>stated</u> or <u>implied</u> in that passage.

Read the following passage:

    John Quincy Adams , who served as the sixth president of the United States from 1825 to 1829, is today recognized for his masterful statesmanship and diplomacy. He dedicated his life to public service, both in the presidency and in the various other political offices he held. Throughout his political career he demonstrated his unswerving belief in freedom of speech, the anti-slavery cause, and the right of Americans to be free from European and Asian domination.

Example I

To what did John Quincy Adams devote his life?

<u>Sample Answer</u>

(A) Improving his personal life
(B) Serving the public
(C) Increasing his fortune
(D) Working on his private business

According to the passage, John Quincy Adams "dedicated his life to public service." Therefore, you should choose answer (B).

GO ON TO THE NEXT PAGE

Example II

The passage implies that John Quincy
Adams held

Ⓐ Ⓑ Ⓒ ●

(A) no political offices
(B) only one political office
(C) exactly two political offices
(D) at least three political offices

The passage states that John Quincy Adams served in "the presidency and various other
political offices." Therefore, you should choose answer (D).

After you read the directions, begin work on the questions.

Questions 31–35

The next famous woman writer to be considered is Dorothy Parker, an American
poet, short story writer, and literary critic who became famous in the early twentieth
century for her witty but cynical observations on life. She got her first paying job as a
writer in 1916 at the age of 23 when she began working for a women's magazine, and
nine years later she became a contributor to *The New Yorker* as a book reviewer.

In addition to her magazine work, she published volumes of poetry and short
stories with the recurrent themes of disappointment with life and the loss of idealism.
One of her most famous observations, "Men seldom make passes/At girls who wear
glasses," came from the poem "News Item," which was published in the volume *Enough
Rope* (1926). This volume of poetry was followed by *Sunset Gin* (1928), *Death and Taxes*
(1931), and a collection of short stories *Here Lies* (1939).

31. According to the passage, Dorothy
Parker was NOT famous for

(A) poetry.
(B) humor.
(C) book reviews.
(D) autobiography.

32. Dorothy Parker's first job was

(A) for a women's magazine
(B) as a literary critic
(C) for *The New Yorker*
(D) as a short story writer

33. In line 7, the word "recurrent" could
best be replaced by which of the
following?

(A) Related
(B) Repeated
(C) Flowing
(D) Negative

34. In what year did "News Item"
appear?

(A) 1916
(B) 1926
(C) 1928
(D) 1931

35. With what topic does the paragraph
preceding the passage most likely
deal?

(A) Dorothy Parker's early
childhood
(B) American literature of the
nineteenth century
(C) An introduction to literary
criticism
(D) A well-known female author
other than Dorothy Parker

GO ON TO THE NEXT PAGE

PRACTICE TEST FIVE

Questions 36–40

Desert tundra, or cold desert, occurs on the Arctic edges of North America, Europe, and Asia. In these areas the near eternal freezing temperatures cause an environment in which plant life is virtually impossible. The existence of ice rather than water for the majority of the year means that vegetation lacks sufficient moisture for growth. During the short period of time when the temperature increases enough for the ice to melt, there is generally a large volume of water. This excess of water, coupled with a lack of drainage through the frozen subsoil, does not allow vegetation to flourish.

36. What would be the most appropriate title for the passage?

   (A) Where Desert Tundra Is Found
   (B) The Weather in the Arctic
   (C) Why Cold Deserts Occur
   (D) The Variety of Plant Life in Desert Tundra

37. According to the passage, desert tundra is found

   (A) throughout North America, Europe, and Asia
   (B) in Antarctica
   (C) on the Arctic borders of the northern continents
   (D) at the North Pole

38. According to the passage, what makes plant life almost impossible in areas of desert tundra during most of the year?

   (A) Excessive water on the plants
   (B) The frozen state of the water
   (C) The increase in temperature
   (D) The lack of ice

39. Which of the following happens when the weather heats up?

   (A) Plants can flourish.
   (B) Vegetation lacks sufficient moisture.
   (C) The days become shorter.
   (D) There is too much water.

40. According to the passage, why can't the water drain after it melts?

   (A) The land beneath the surface is still frozen.
   (B) The temperature is too high.
   (C) The period of time is too short.
   (D) The vegetation is flourishing.

GO ON TO THE NEXT PAGE

Questions 41–44

It is the role of the Federal Reserve, known simply as the Fed, to control the supply of money in the U.S. through its system of twelve regional Federal Reserve Banks, each with its own Federal Reserve District Bank. Many commercial banks belong to the Federal Reserve System and as members must follow the Fed's reserve requirements, a ruling by the Fed on the percentage of deposits that a member bank must keep either in its own vaults or on deposit at the Fed. If the Fed wants to change the money supply, it can change reserve requirements to member banks; for example, an increase in the percentage of deposits required to be kept on hand would reduce the available money supply. Member banks can also borrow money from the Fed, and an additional way that the Fed can control the money supply is to raise or lower the discount rate, the interest rate at which commercial banks borrow from the Fed. An increase in the discount rate would reduce the funds available to commercial banks and thus shrink the money supply. In addition to using reserve requirements and the discount rate to control the money supply, the Fed has an additional powerful tool: open-market operations.

41. According to the passage, the main purpose of the Federal Reserve System is to

(A) increase reserve requirements
(B) increase or decrease the amount of money available
(C) increase the number of Federal Reserve Banks
(D) increase the money kept on deposit by member banks

42. When the Fed controls the percentage of deposits kept on hand by member banks, it controls

(A) district banks
(B) the discount rate
(C) the reserve requirement
(D) borrowing by commercial banks

43. The passage implies that a lowering of the discount rate would lead to

(A) an increase in the money supply
(B) a decrease in borrowing from the Fed by commercial banks
(C) a decrease in the money available
(D) an increase in the reserve requirement

44. The paragraph following the passage most likely discusses

(A) the need for controlling the money supply
(B) the structure of the Federal Reserve System
(C) recent changes in reserve requirements
(D) open-market purchases and sales

GO ON TO THE NEXT PAGE

Questions 45–49

Fog occurs when damp air above the surface of the earth is cooled to the point at which it condenses. Of the two types of fog, advection fog occurs along the ocean coast or near rivers or lakes. This type of fast-moving fog, which may cover vast areas, occurs when warm winds blow across a cold surface of land or water. In this collision of heat and cold, the warm air is cooled to the point at which the water vapor condenses into fog. Radiation fog, quite different from advection fog, is immobile cloud-like moisture generally found hovering over wintertime valleys. It occurs on clear nights when the earth's warmth escapes into the upper atmosphere.

45. According to the passage, fog is found when wetness in the air is

   (A) vaporized
   (B) cooled
   (C) dampened
   (D) heated

46. According to the passage, advection fog is found

   (A) in valleys
   (B) in the ocean
   (C) near bodies of water
   (D) only in small, enclosed areas

47. In the passage, radiation fog is said to be

   (A) similar to advection fog
   (B) found in coastal areas
   (C) fast-moving
   (D) trapped moisture hanging over inland valleys

48. According to the passage, which of the following statements about fog is true?

   (A) Advection fog is caused when cold winds blow across a heated land surface.
   (B) Advection fog is the type of fog that occurs in small valleys on clear nights.
   (C) Radiation fog occurs when the cooled atmosphere meets with heat from the earth.
   (D) Radiation fog generally moves quickly across vast areas of land.

49. The author's purpose in this passage is to

   (A) explain the different types of fog
   (B) describe where different types of fog are found
   (C) discuss advection fog
   (D) give a scientific description of various types of precipitation

GO ON TO THE NEXT PAGE

Questions 50–54

It is a strong belief among certain groups of people that the medical community should take every possible step to keep a person alive, without regard for the quality of that person's life. But other people argue just as strongly that patients who are facing a life of pain and incumberance on others have the right to decide for themselves whether or not to continue with life-prolonging medications and therapies.

The question, however, is really far more difficult than just the issue of a terminally ill patient of sound mind who directs the physician not to continue with any treatment that does not in any way cure the disease but only helps to draw out a painful death. When the quality of life has disintegrated, when there is no hope of reprieve, when there is intense and everpresent pain, does the patient have the right to be put to death? The patient in this case is not asking the physician to discontinue treatment but instead is requesting the physician, the supposed protector of life, to purposefully bring a life to a close.

50. With what subject is the passage mainly concerned?

   (A) Community beliefs
   (B) Ways to prolong life
   (C) The right to die
   (D) The role of the physician

51. The phrase "medical community" (sentence 1) means

   (A) the area around a hospital
   (B) medicines and therapies
   (C) doctors and nurses
   (D) medical journals

52. "However", as it is used in the first sentence of the second paragraph, could best be replaced by which of the following?

   (A) On the contrary
   (B) Thus
   (C) In effect
   (D) Certainly

53. In what situation does the author suggest that a patient might have the right to be put to death?

   (A) When the patient is of sound mind
   (B) When pain has disintegrated
   (C) At the request of the physician
   (D) When the patient is facing great pain and inevitable death

54. Which of the following statements best applies to the idea presented in the passage?

   (A) The question of a patient's right to die is rarely faced by physicians.
   (B) The author firmly states his opinion on the right to die.
   (C) All people are in agreement as to a patient's right to die.
   (D) Putting a patient to death is more serious than allowing a patient to die.

Questions 55–60

A binary star is actually a pair of stars that are held together by the force of gravity. Although occasionally the individual stars that compose a binary star can be distinguished, they generally appear as one star. The gravitational pull between the individual stars of a binary star causes one to orbit around the other. From the orbital pattern of a binary, the mass of its stars can be determined: the gravitational pull of a star is in direct proportion to its mass, and the strength of the gravitational force of one star on another determines the orbital pattern of the binary. Scientists have discovered

PRACTICE TEST FIVE

GO ON TO THE NEXT PAGE

stars that seem to orbit around an empty space. It has been suggested that such a star and the empty space really compose a binary star. The empty space is known as a *black hole*, a star with such a strong gravitational force that no light is able to get through.

55. A binary star could best be described as

    (A) stars that have been forced apart
    (B) a star with a strong gravitational force
    (C) two stars pulled together by gravity
    (D) a large number of attached stars

56. According to the passage, what happens as a result of the gravitational force between the stars?

    (A) One star circles the other.
    (B) The mass of the binary star increases.
    (C) A black hole is destroyed.
    (D) The gravitational force decreases.

57. According to the passage, what can scientists learn from the pattern of a binary star's orbit?

    (A) The proportion of the star's gravitational pull to its mass
    (B) How to distinguish the stars that compose a binary
    (C) Why there is no light in a *black hole*
    (D) The mass of the stars that compose the binary

58. According to the passage, what is a *black hole?*

    (A) An empty space around which nothing orbits
    (B) A star with close to zero gravity
    (C) A star whose gravitational force blocks the passage of light
    (D) An empty space so far away that no light can reach it

59. Which of the following statements about *black holes* is NOT true?

    (A) A *black hole* can have a star orbiting around it.
    (B) A binary star can be composed of a *black hole* and a visible star.
    (C) All empty space contains *black holes.*
    (D) The gravitational pull of a *black hole* is strong.

60. This passage would most likely be assigned reading in a course on

    (A) botany
    (B) astrophysics
    (C) geology
    (D) astrology

THIS IS THE END OF SECTION 3

IF YOU FINISH BEFORE TIME IS CALLED, CHECK YOUR WORK
ON SECTION 3 ONLY.
DO NOT READ OR WORK ON ANY OTHER SECTION OF THE TEST.

SECTION
TEST OF WRITTEN ENGLISH: ESSAY QUESTION
Time—30 minutes

Some citizens are strongly in favor of the development of nuclear power, but others argue that nuclear power is a clear danger to life on earth. Discuss both positions. Then indicate which you agree with and why.

Write your answer on the answer sheet for the Test of Written English, Practice Test Five, on pages 185–186.

PRACTICE TEST ONE TAPESCRIPT

SECTION 1
LISTENING COMPREHENSION

In this section of the test, you will have an opportunity to demonstrate your ability to understand spoken English. There are three parts in this section, with special directions for each part.

Part A

Directions: For each question in Part A, you will hear a short sentence. Each sentence will be spoken just one time. The sentences you hear will not be written out for you. Therefore, you must listen carefully to understand what the speaker says.

After you hear a sentence, read the four choices in your test book, marked (A), (B), (C), and (D), and decide which one is closest in meaning to the sentence you heard. Then, on your answer sheet, find the number of the question and fill in the space that corresponds to the letter of the answer you have chosen. Fill in the space so the letter inside the oval cannot be seen.

Example I

You will hear:
   John was the fastest runner in the race.

You will read:
   (A) John outran the others.
   (B) John was the fastest hunter in the chase.
   (C) John wasn't the slowest in the race.
   (D) John was the last runner to finish the race.

The speaker said, "John was the fastest runner in the race." Sentence (A), "John outran the others," is closest in meaning to the sentence you heard. Therefore, you should choose answer (A).

Example II

You will hear:
   Could you help me move my desk?

You will read:
   (A) Could you help me use the rest?
   (B) Do you mind using the other desk?
   (C) Would you mind helping me carry this piece of furniture?
   (D) If you move my desk, I'll help you with your work.

The speaker said, "Could you help me move my desk?" Sentence (C), "Would you mind helping me carry this piece of furniture?" is closest in meaning to the sentence you heard. Therefore, you should choose answer (C).

1. In rainy weather, there are many car accidents.
2. Thomas passed his comprehensive exams a week ago.
3. I forgot to announce the meeting.
4. This book isn't due for a week.
5. Sue worked as a saleswoman during Christmas vacation.
6. We flew to San Francisco just to see our grandparents.
7. The administration building is next to the bookstore, isn't it?
8. It was impossible to find a place to park before class at 10:00.
9. Debbie's purse is still here, so she must still be in the apartment.
10. She can't seem to find the magazine.
11. Mary followed the directions to the letter.
12. How nice of them to invite you there for dinner.
13. I rarely take vacations from work.
14. The lawyer prepared hard for the case, but his work was for nothing.
15. The movie couldn't have been any funnier.

16. George will pass the class providing he submits his paper in time.

17. They shouldn't wait to pay the bills.

18. The university has plans to build a new athletic field.

19. Paul was able to overturn the board's decision.

20. The researcher isn't at all dissatisfied with his findings.

Part B

Directions: In Part B you will hear short conversations between two speakers. At the end of each conversation, a third person will ask a question about what was said. You will hear each conversation and question about it just one time. Therefore, you must listen carefully to understand what each speaker says. After you hear a conversation and the question about it, read the four possible answers in your test book and decide which one is the best answer to the question you heard. Then, on your answer sheet, find the number of the question and fill in the space that corresponds to the letter of the answer you have chosen.

Look at the following example.

You will hear:
    Man: That exam was just awful.
Woman: Oh, it could have been worse.
      Q: What does the woman mean?

You will read:
  (A) The exam was really awful.
  (B) It was the worst exam she had ever seen.
  (C) It couldn't have been more difficult.
  (D) It wasn't that hard.

From the conversation you learn that the man thought the exam was very difficult and that the woman disagreed with the man. The best answer to the question "What does the woman mean?" is (D), "It wasn't that hard." Therefore, you should choose answer (D).

21. **Man:** This television cost me fifty dollars.
   Woman: Only fifty dollars? Mine cost a fortune.
      Q: What does the woman mean?

22. **Woman:** Bob, what are you doing with that budgetary report?
   Man: I keep adding and readding the numbers, but they just don't balance.
      Q: What is Bob's profession most likely to be?

23. **Man:** Did you get the tickets?
   Woman: Yes, I did. Let's go on in because the film's about to start.
      Q: Where does this conversation probably take place?

24. **Man:** Is there any more typing paper?
   Woman: Not that I know of.
      Q: What does the woman mean?

25. **Woman:** I'd like to see the personnel director, please.
   Man: He'll be in tomorrow at 10:00. Would you like to make an appointment?
      Q: What will the woman probably do?

26. **Man:** Have you seen the school play?
   Woman: Seen it? I have the lead role.
      Q: What does the woman mean?

27. **Man:** I don't know if Steve liked the apartment or not.
   Woman: He said he liked it, but then he didn't want to sign the lease.
      Q: What can be concluded about Steve?

28. **Woman:** Sally just arrived at the airport.
   Man: And not a minute too soon.
      Q: What does the man mean?

29. **Man:** Will this take very long? I have to drive my children to school.
   Woman: Well, you need to have your teeth cleaned and a cavity filled.
      Q: Where does this conversation probably take place?

30. **First
Woman:** Can I borrow your blue sweater, Alice?
   **Second
Woman:** Only if you promise to return it tomorrow.
   Q: What does Alice say about the sweater?

31. **Woman:** Been working long?
   Man: Not really. Only since last week.
   Q: What does the man mean?

32. **Man:** Lucky Tom. He just bought a new car.
   Woman: Lucky? He had to buy it because he wrecked his other car in an accident.
   Q: What does the woman mean?

33. **Woman:** I can't believe that it's snowing again today.
   Man: Two weeks without a change is pretty boring.
   Q: What does the man mean?

34. **Man:** The bookstore's out of the texts for American history, and the first exam is next week.
   Woman: You'd better borrow one from a friend, because the new order won't arrive by then.
   Q: What does the woman mean?

35. **Man:** There's a symphony concert tomorrow night. Do you want to go with me?
   Woman: What a good idea! I haven't been to one in a long time.
   Q: What will the woman probably do?

Part C

Directions: In this part of the test, you will hear short talks and conversations. After each of them, you will be asked some questions. You will hear the talks and conversations and the questions about them just one time. They will not be written out for you. Therefore, you must listen carefully to understand what each speaker says.

After you hear a question, read the four possible answers in your test book and decide which one is the best answer to the question you heard. Then, on your answer sheet, find the number of the question and fill in the space that corresponds to the letter of the answer you have chosen.

Listen to this sample talk.

You will hear:
   Artist Grant Wood was a guiding force in the school of painting known as American regionalist, a style reflecting the distinctive characteristics of art from rural areas of the United States. Wood began drawing animals on the family farm at the age of three, and when he was thirty-eight one of his paintings received a remarkable amount of public notice and acclaim. This painting, called *American Gothic*, is a starkly simple depiction of a serious couple staring directly out at the viewer.

Now look at the following example.

You will hear:
   What style of painting is known as American regionalist?

You will read:
   (A) Art from America's inner cities.
   (B) Art from the central region of the U.S.
   (C) Art from various urban areas in the U.S.
   (D) Art from rural sections of America.

The best answer to the question "What style of painting is known as American regionalist?" is (D), "Art from rural sections of America." Therefore, you should choose answer (D).

Now look at the next example.

You will hear:
   What is the name of Wood's most successful painting?

You will read:
   (A) *American Regionalist.*
   (B) *The Family Farm in Iowa.*
   (C) *American Gothic.*
   (D) *A Serious Couple.*

The best answer to the question "What is the name of Wood's most successful painting?" is (C), "*American Gothic.*" Therefore, you should choose answer (C).

PRACTICE TEST ONE TAPESCRIPT

Questions 36 through 41 are based on the following conversation.

Woman: Have you started your research project for management class?

Man: Well, I've decided on a topic: I want to write about motivation. But I haven't actually started the research yet.

Woman: When are you going to begin the research? You don't have that much time to complete the paper.

Man: I went to the library, but I wasn't sure where to look.

Woman: Well, you can try the card catalog if you want to find books about motivation.

Man: The professor said that we shouldn't use just books as references for our papers. We should also use journal articles as references. Would I find those in the card catalog also?

Woman: No, for journal articles you should look in an index for journal articles. There's an index for almost every subject. I'm sure there's an index for management topics.

Man: Well, I guess I should get started today. I think I'll head to the library now. Thanks for your help.

36. What is the topic of this conversation?
37. Why has the man not completed the research?
38. According to the woman, where should the man look to find books about motivation?
39. What types of resources should the man use in his research project?
40. Which of the following could the man probably find in an index?
41. What will the man probably do next?

Questions 42 through 46 are based on the following talk.

Up to now in this course on American authors we have studied American novelists, but next class we will move on to short story writers. We will begin with a man who is probably the most famous American short story writer of all, Edgar Allen Poe. To truly understand an author, it is important to have knowledge of events in his life and times and how they affected his works. In Poe's case, we will see that the major tragedies in his life, particularly the untimely death of his wife after a long illness, exerted a major influence on his work. In addition to studying Poe's life and times, we will read several of his short stories, including "The Fall of the House of Usher" and "The Masque of the Red Death," and write a short analysis of one of the stories. Poe is best known for his symbolism, his impressionistic style, and his ability to create and maintain an eerie tone, and those two short stories are excellent examples of his style. For the next class, you should read "The Fall of the House of Usher" thoroughly, and be prepared for a discussion.

42. In which course does this talk probably take place?
43. What subject have the students just finished studying?
44. According to the speaker, what kind of life did Poe have?
45. Which of the following is not a characteristic of Poe's work?
46. What should the students do to prepare for the next class?

Questions 47 through 50 are based on the following talk.

Sign language, an Indian language based on hand movements, developed from a need to improve communications among the Plains Indians of North America. There were many different Indian tribes on the plains of North America, and each tribe had its own language. Because these tribes often came into contact, there was a strong need to develop some form of communication. Sign language arose from this need. With sign language, Indians who spoke widely differing languages were able to communicate at least on a basic level, by gesturing with their hands.

47. What is sign language?
48. Why did sign language develop?
49. How often did various tribes meet?
50. How could sign language be characterized?

PRACTICE TEST TWO TAPESCRIPT

SECTION 1
LISTENING COMPREHENSION

In this section of the test, you will have an opportunity to demonstrate your ability to understand spoken English. There are three parts in this section, with special directions for each part.

Part A

Directions: For each question in Part A, you will hear a short sentence. Each sentence will be spoken just one time. The sentences you hear will not be written out for you. Therefore, you must listen carefully to understand what the speaker says.

After you hear a sentence, read the four choices in your test book, marked (A), (B), (C), and (D), and decide which one is closest in meaning to the sentence you heard. Then, on your answer sheet, find the number of the question and fill in the space that corresponds to the letter of the answer you have chosen. Fill in the space so the letter inside the oval cannot be seen.

Example I

You will hear:
John was the fastest runner in the race.

You will read:
(A) John outran the others.
(B) John was the fastest hunter in the chase.
(C) John wasn't the slowest in the race.
(D) John was the last runner to finish the race.

The speaker said, "John was the fastest runner in the race." Sentence (A), "John outran the others," is closest in meaning to the sentence you heard. Therefore, you should choose answer (A).

Example II

You will hear:
Could you help me move my desk?

You will read:
(A) Could you help me use the rest?
(B) Do you mind using the other desk?
(C) Would you mind helping me carry this piece of furniture?
(D) If you move my desk, I'll help you with your work.

The speaker said, "Could you help me move my desk?" Sentence (C), "Would you mind helping me carry this piece of furniture?" is closest in meaning to the sentence you heard. Therefore, you should choose answer (C).

1. Whatever movie you choose, I'll be happy to see it.
2. Maria took their order, brought them coffee, and served the meal.
3. The copy machine's next to the encyclopedia table.
4. The motorist has overtaken the train.
5. Pat doesn't mind doing the laundry, nor does Jim.
6. She prefers not to work on group projects.
7. No doubt Bill's portfolio was the biggest.
8. Aren't the roses beautiful!
9. Jane has a cousin in San Francisco, so she often goes there during the holidays.
10. The woman was disturbed by the noisy traffic.
11. You went to that restaurant just last week?
12. Margaret looked up the definition in the unabridged dictionary.
13. She lacks the ability to complete the exercise.
14. Even as we speak, Mark's trying to compute the answers to his math problems on his calculator.
15. The exams will be corrected by noon.
16. Mike was named to the student council.

17. You'd better hurry. Take five minutes too long and you'll miss the bus.
18. Bill gives priority to extremely sick patients.
19. Even though spring's a few weeks away, it's quite warm today.
20. I couldn't believe that he was unprepared.

Part B

Directions: In Part B you will hear short conversations between two speakers. At the end of each conversation, a third person will ask a question about what was said. You will hear each conversation and question about it just one time. Therefore, you must listen carefully to understand what each speaker says. After you hear a conversation and the question about it, read the four possible answers in your test book and decide which one is the best answer to the question you heard. Then, on your answer sheet, find the number of the question and fill in the space that corresponds to the letter of the answer you have chosen.

Look at the following example.

You will hear:
Man: That exam was just awful.
Woman: Oh, it could have been worse.
Q: What does the woman mean?

You will read:
(A)   The exam was really awful.
(B)   It was the worst exam she had ever seen.
(C)   It couldn't have been more difficult.
(D)   It wasn't that hard.

From the conversation you learn that the man thought the exam was very difficult and that the woman disagreed with the man. The best answer to the question "What does the woman mean?" is (D), "It wasn't that hard." Therefore, you should choose answer (D).

21.   Man: I found my briefcase.
    Woman: Just a moment. That's my briefcase. Yours is smaller, isn't it?
    Q: What does the woman mean?

22.   Woman: The history assignment was difficult. I worked all night and couldn't finish it.
    Man: You worked all night? It took me only thirty minutes.
    Q: Why is the man surprised?

23.   Man: Would you like me to get you some coffee?
    Woman: Not now, thanks. Maybe later.
    Q: What does the woman want?

24.   Man: Let's go for a walk at the beach today.
    Woman: Why not? It's too nice to stay indoors.
    Q: What does the woman mean?

25.   Woman: Can I still get dinner in the cafeteria tonight?
    Man: If you get in line quickly.
    Q: What will probably happen soon?

26.   Man: That's a nice cake. Did you make it yourself?
    Woman: Not exactly. My roommate helped with the frosting.
    Q: What does the woman mean?

27.   Man: Would you tell me what time the dormitory doors will be locked?
    Woman: No problem. In fact, I can give you a copy of the dormitory rulebook.
    Q: What does the man want to know?

28.   Woman: Was Roger upset when he heard the news?
    Man: Oh, he really fell apart!
    Q: How did Roger feel?

29.   Man: I've run out of time. Can we finish this problem tomorrow?
    Woman: Great. I'll see you then.
    Q: What is the man's problem?

30.   Woman: How much of a tip should we leave?
    Man: Not more than a dollar. The service was slow and the soup was cold.
    Q: Where does this conversation probably take place?

31. **Woman:** Wasn't the anthropology lecture fascinating?
    Man: Fascinating? It was too long and drawn out for me.
    Q: How did the man feel about the lecture?

32. **Woman:** Are there enough drinks in the refrigerator?
    Man: Enough? Any more and we'll need another refrigerator.
    Q: What does the man mean?

33. **Man:** Have you completed the paper for history class?
    Woman: No, I can't seem to get things done in time.
    Q: What does the woman mean?

34. **Woman:** Hey, George. Did the student council come to a decision on the parking issue?
    Man: No, it was put off until next week.
    Q: What happened in this situation?

35. **Man:** Are you attending the planning committee meeting later?
    Woman: Only if I have to.
    Q: What does the woman mean?

Part C

Directions: In this part of the test, you will hear short talks and conversations. After each of them, you will be asked some questions. You will hear the talks and conversations and the questions about them just one time. They will not be written out for you. Therefore, you must listen carefully to understand what each speaker says.

After you hear a question, read the four possible answers in your test book and decide which one is the best answer to the question you heard. Then, on your answer sheet, find the number of the question and fill in the space that corresponds to the letter of the answer you have chosen.

Listen to this sample talk.

You will hear:
   Artist Grant Wood was a guiding force in the school of painting known as American regionalist, a style reflecting the distinctive characteristics of art from rural areas of the United States. Wood began drawing animals on the family farm at the age of three, and when he was thirty-eight one of his paintings received a remarkable amount of public notice and acclaim. This painting, called *American Gothic*, is a starkly simple depiction of a serious couple staring directly out at the viewer.

Now look at the following example.

You will hear:
   What style of painting is known as American regionalist?

You will read:
   (A) Art from America's inner cities.
   (B) Art from the central region of the U.S.
   (C) Art from the various urban areas in the U.S.
   (D) Art from rural sections of America.

The best answer to the question "What style of painting is known as American regionalist?" is (D), "Art from rural sections of America." Therefore, you should choose answer (D).

Now look at the next example.

You will hear:
   What is the name of Wood's most successful painting?

You will read:
   (A) *American Regionalist.*
   (B) *The Family Farm in Iowa.*
   (C) *American Gothic.*
   (D) *A Serious Couple.*

The best answer to the question "What is the name of Wood's most successful painting?" is (C), "*American Gothic.*" Therefore, you should choose answer (C).

Questions 36 through 40 are based on the following conversation.

Man: Hey, Gloria. How would you like to increase the extent of your educational and historical background?
Woman: Steve, I don't understand what you're saying at all.

Man: I just took my final in History 101 this morning, and I'm trying to get rid of the books. They cost $80.

Woman: Why don't you try to sell them back to the bookstore?

Man: I tried, but they'd only refund $20, and I paid so much more for them. I'd like to get at least $40.

Woman: Well, I'm not going to take History 101, so I'm not really interested in those books. Maybe you should ask some other friends.

Man: I already have. Everyone I know has already taken History 101 and doesn't want those books.

Woman: Why don't you put up some advertisements in the history building? Maybe someone you don't know will call you and buy them.

Man: I'll try it, but I don't think that'll work.

Woman: Then you'll have to go back to the bookstore. Twenty dollars is better than nothing.

36. Where does this conversation probably take place?
37. What is the topic of this conversation?
38. Why is the man interested in selling his books?
39. Why does the man not want to sell the books to the bookstore?
40. What does the woman suggest that the man do?

Questions 41 through 45 are based on the following talk.

The importance to the United States of the first transcontinental railroad cannot be overrated. This railroad had a profound effect on many aspects of American life, on communication, on transportation of agricultural products and livestock to market, and on the settlement of the West, to name a few. But it was no easy feat to build such a railroad. The first transcontinental railroad was undertaken in 1862 by two competing railroad companies. The Union Pacific started in Omaha, Nebraska, and moved westward; the Central Pacific began in Sacramento, California, and moved eastward. Of the two, the Central Pacific had the more difficult task because it was faced with traversing the Sierra Nevadas. To lay tracks across these mountains, workers had to carve out footpaths on steep mountain faces and then use dynamite to blast out access for the railroad tracks. After years of dangerous and exhausting labor, the workers from the Central Pacific met up with the workers from the Union Pacific near Ogden, Utah, on May 10, 1869. In an exuberant ceremony, the last of the tracks was nailed to the ground with a golden spike. The completion of the railroad marked the beginning of a new era in transportation.

41. Who built the first transcontinental railroad?
42. What was difficult about the job the Central Pacific workers had to complete?
43. How is the job of a railroad worker described?
44. How long did it take to complete the first transcontinental railroad?
45. What happened at the ceremony marking the completion of the railroad?

Questions 46 through 50 are based on the following conversation.

Man: I was reading in last night's paper that the utility company wants to build a solar energy plant in the desert not far from here.

Woman: Do you think that's a good idea?

Man: A good idea? It's a great idea! Solar energy is the energy of the future. It's clean, it's safe, and it's abundant. What could be better?

Woman: Won't the utility company just raise our rates to pay for this new plant?

Man: The newspaper said that the utility company will need extra money to get the plant going, but in the long run rates will be lower. And to have a constant supply of energy, that's a small price to pay.

Woman: I'm not convinced that the price will be so small.

46. How did the man learn about the new solar energy plant?
47. Where will the solar energy plant be constructed?
48. According to the man, what are the benefits of solar energy?
49. How does the man feel about the cost of the plant?
50. How does the woman feel about the proposed solar energy plant?

PRACTICE TEST THREE TAPESCRIPT

SECTION 1
LISTENING COMPREHENSION

In this section of the test, you will have an opportunity to demonstrate your ability to understand spoken English. There are three parts in this section, with special directions for each part.

Part A

<u>Directions:</u>   For each question in Part A, you will hear a short sentence. Each sentence will be spoken just one time. The sentences you hear will not be written out for you. Therefore, you must listen carefully to understand what the speaker says.

After you hear a sentence, read the four choices in your test book, marked (A), (B), (C), and (D), and decide which <u>one</u> is closest in meaning to the sentence <u>you</u> heard. Then, on your answer sheet, find the number of the question and fill in the space that corresponds to the letter of the answer you have chosen. Fill in the space so the letter inside the oval cannot be seen.

Example I

You will hear:
    John was the fastest runner in the race.

You will read:
    (A) John outran the others.
    (B) John was the fastest hunter in the chase.
    (C) John wasn't the slowest in the race.
    (D) John was the last runner to finish the race.

The speaker said, "John was the fastest runner in the race." Sentence (A), "John outran the others," is closest in meaning to the sentence you heard. Therefore, you should choose answer (A).

Example II

You will hear:
    Could you help me move my desk?

You will read:
    (A) Could you help me use the rest?
    (B) Do you mind using the other desk?
    (C) Would you mind helping me carry this piece of furniture?
    (D) If you move my desk, I'll help you with your work.

The speaker said, "Could you help me move my desk?" Sentence (C), "Would you mind helping me carry this piece of furniture?" is closest in meaning to the sentence you heard. Therefore, you should choose answer (C).

1. When's your flight?
2. The room was bigger than necessary.
3. The teacher said that the students should read one chapter per week.
4. Bob told us that the library opened at 10:00.
5. I made Sally finish the assignment.
6. After a student finishes the required courses, he can take three electives.
7. Martha, who's a marine biologist, led a seminar on the migration of whales.
8. Under no circumstances does the dean listen to any complaints.
9. Mark studied thoroughly for the exam, and Amy did too.
10. The building might be started next month.
11. Well, don't you think this lunch is delicious?
12. He should check off the names of the students who have completed the assignment.
13. We haven't seen rain like this for many years.

14. In the nick of time she swerved and missed the truck.

15. The lawyer sat her down and broke the news.

16. Suzanne bought a stunning new dress for the party.

17. For an additional fee, the agency will add another city to the tour.

18. The child ran out of the room, too frightened to stay any longer.

19. There's a wide selection of shoes at the mall.

20. He's yet to attend a seminar.

Part B

Look at the following example.

You will hear:
    Man: That exam was just awful.
  Woman: Oh, it could have been worse.
      Q: What does the woman mean?

You will read:
(A) The exam was really awful.
(B) It was the worst exam she had ever seen.
(C) It couldn't have been more difficult.
(D) It wasn't that hard.

From the conversation you learn that the man thought the exam was very difficult and that the woman disagreed with the man. The best answer to the question "What does the woman mean?" is (D), "It wasn't that hard." Therefore, you should choose answer (D).

21. **Woman:** Can we sit anywhere?
   Man: No, this section is reserved.
     Q: What does the man mean?

22. **Woman:** I'm ready for the therapy session.
   Man: Would you mind taking a seat?
     Q: What does the man want her to do?

23. **Woman:** Have you finished washing the dishes?
   Man: I've been working on my term paper instead.
     Q: What does the man mean?

24. **Woman:** I'm leaving for New York tomorrow at noon. Could you take me to the airport?
   Man: Sorry. I'm working then. Why not see if Mike can help you out?
     Q: What does the man suggest?

25.   **Man:** How can I finish all these problems before midnight?
 Woman: Why not leave some for the morning?
     Q: What does the woman suggest?

26. **Woman:** Can you turn off the lights when you leave?
   Man: No problem. Our utility bill is high enough as it is.
     Q: What is the man concerned about?

27. **Woman:** Have you seen the announcement in the lobby?
   Man: What announcement is that?
     Q: What does the man mean?

28.   **Man:** Why don't we shut down for tonight? It's late.
 Woman: Shut down? But we have so much more to do.
     Q: What does the woman mean?

29.   **Man:** Is the lecture tonight worth watching?
 Woman: Without a doubt!
     Q: What does the woman say about the lecture?

30. **Woman:** The anthem just finished and the game's about to start.
   Man: Let's get drinks later, then.
     Q: What does the man probably want to do?

31. **Woman:** Do you think we should bring the camera with us?
     Man: That doesn't sound like a bad idea.
     Q: What does the man mean?

32. **Man:** The prices on this airline are a little high, don't you think?
     Woman: They seem reasonable, for a trip to the moon.
     Q: What does the woman mean?

33. **Woman:** It never occurred to me that you were an athlete.
     Man: Most people who meet me don't think so, either.
     Q: What can be said about the man?

34. **Man:** Can we meet later to work on our presentation?
     Woman: How about noon?
     Q: What does the woman mean?

35. **Woman:** Why don't we spend our vacation in the Bahamas?
     Man: I don't make enough to do that.
     Q: What does the man mean?

Part C

Directions: In this part of the test, you will hear short talks and conversations. After each of them, you will be asked some questions. You will hear the talks and conversations and the questions about them just one time. They will not be written out for you. Therefore, you must listen carefully to understand what each speaker says.

After you hear a question, read the four possible answers in your test book and decide which one is the best answer to the question you heard. Then, on your answer sheet, find the number of the question and fill in the space that corresponds to the letter of the answer you have chosen.

Listen to this sample talk.

You will hear:
  Artist Grant Wood was a guiding force in the school of painting known as American regionalist, a style reflecting the distinctive characteristics of art from rural areas of the United States. Wood began drawing animals on the family farm at the age of three, and when he was thirty-eight one of his paintings received a remarkable amount of public notice and acclaim. This painting, called *American Gothic*, is a starkly simple depiction of a serious couple staring directly out at the viewer.

Now look at the following example.

You will hear:
  What style of painting is known as American regionalist?

You will read:
  (A) Art from America's inner cities.
  (B) Art from the central region of the U.S.
  (C) Art from various urban areas in the U.S.
  (D) Art from rural sections of America.

The best answer to the question "What style of painting is known as American regionalist?" is (D), "Art from rural sections of America." Therefore, you should choose answer (D).

Now look at the next example.

You will hear:
  What is the name of Wood's most successful painting?

You will read:
  (A) *American Regionalist.*
  (B) *The Family Farm in Iowa.*
  (C) *American Gothic.*
  (D) *A Serious Couple.*

The best answer to the question "What is the name of Wood's most successful painting?" is (C), "*American Gothic.*" Therefore, you should choose answer (C).

Questions 36 through 40 are based on the following conversation.

  Man: Dora, could you give me some help?
  Woman: With what?
  Man: I kept putting off my History 101 paper, and it's due next week.
  Woman: If you want to pass the course, you've got to write that paper.

Man: I know. I thought that since you're a history major, you could help me come up with a topic for my paper.

Woman: History 101 is about American History. You could write about the Revolutionary War, or the Civil War, or World War I.

Man: Oh, I don't want to write about wars. I don't want to think about killing and death. Can you think of something else?

Woman: Why don't you write about technology, inventions that changed American history?

Man: That topic seems a little broad. Maybe I should narrow it down a bit.

Woman: Well, you could choose one invention, the telephone or the airplane for example, and write about its effect on history.

Man: I know. My favorite topic is cars. I'll write about the invention of the automobile and its effect on American history.

Woman: That sounds like a good topic for you. Now you'd better get busy. You only have one week.

36.   What does the man ask the woman to do?
37.   When in the semester does this conversation probably take place?
38.   What course is the man taking this semester?
39.   Why won't the man choose "technology" for a topic?
40.   How much time does the man have to write the paper?

Questions 41 through 44 are based on the following talk.

The development of the radio into a worldwide force occurred relatively quickly. In 1920, only nineteen years after Marconi sent the first wireless signal across the Atlantic, the world's first radio station was established in Pittsburgh, Pennsylvania, and by 1923 nationwide broadcasting was possible in the United States. Radio broadcasting was initially totally uncontrolled, and each of the dozens of existing stations broadcasted its programs whenever and on whatever wavelength it wanted. The result for listeners, as you can imagine, was often a garbled mess. This confused situation in radio broadcasting lasted until the Federal Communications Commission, which is often referred to as the FCC, was created in 1930 by the United States government. The initial purpose of the FCC was to regulate radio broadcasting; each station was assigned a wavelength for its broadcasts to minimize interference from other radio stations.

41.   What is the topic of this talk?
42.   This lecture would probably be given in which of the following courses?
43.   Which of the following best describes the situation in early radio broadcasting?
44.   What do the initials FCC stand for?

Questions 45 through 50 are based on the following talk.

I hope you've enjoyed your visit so far in Washington, D.C. Today, we're going on a tour of the Smithsonian. The Smithsonian is actually several museums, each with a different focus, situated together on a mall. These museums in total have more than sixty million items on exhibit. The first Smithsonian museum we'll visit is the Museum of Natural History, which has various types of stuffed animals and exhibits showing the lifestyles of early American Indians and Eskimos. From the Museum of Natural History, we'll go on to the National Air and Space Museum, where we'll see displays that show the development of flight. In this museum you can see the airplane that Orville Wright used to make his first flight and the airplane that Charles Lindbergh used to cross the Atlantic. After we visit those two museums as a group, you'll have free time to visit some of the other Smithsonian museums: the Museum of American History, the Smithsonian Arts and Industries Building, and the various art museums located on the Smithsonian Mall. After our trip to the Smithsonian today, we'll go on to the White House and Capitol Building tomorrow.

45.   Who is probably giving this talk?
46.   How many items are on exhibit in the Smithsonian museums?
47.   According to the passage, which museum has exhibits of early Eskimos?
48.   Which museum will they visit as a group?
49.   According to the speaker, when is it possible for the tour members to go to an art museum?
50.   Where will they go tomorrow?

PRACTICE TEST FOUR TAPESCRIPT

SECTION 1
LISTENING COMPREHENSION

In this section of the test, you will have an opportunity to demonstrate your ability to understand spoken English. There are three parts in this section, with special directions for each part.

Part A

Directions: For each question in Part A, you will hear a short sentence. Each sentence will be spoken just one time. The sentences you hear will not be written out for you. Therefore, you must listen carefully to understand what the speaker says.

After you hear a sentence, read the four choices in your test book, marked (A), (B), (C), and (D), and decide which one is closest in meaning to the sentence you heard. Then, on your answer sheet, find the number of the question and fill in the space that corresponds to the letter of the answer you have chosen. Fill in the space so the letter inside the oval cannot be seen.

Example I

You will hear:
    John was the fastest runner in the race.

You will read:
    (A) John outran the others.
    (B) John was the fastest hunter in the chase.
    (C) John wasn't the slowest in the race.
    (D) John was the last runner to finish the race.

The speaker said, "John was the fastest runner in the race." Sentence (A), "John outran the others," is closest in meaning to the sentence you heard. Therefore, you should choose answer (A).

Example II

You will hear:
    Could you help me move my desk?

You will read:
    (A) Could you help me use the rest?
    (B) Do you mind using the other desk?
    (C) Would you mind helping me carry this piece of furniture?
    (D) If you move my desk, I'll help you with your work.

The speaker said, "Could you help me move my desk?" Sentence (C), "Would you mind helping me carry this piece of furniture?" is closest in meaning to the sentence you heard. Therefore, you should choose answer (C).

1. The city bus is rather expensive, don't you think?
2. She moved her desk so that she could see the blackboard.
3. Nothing's more important to me than this class.
4. How difficult this assignment is!
5. She ought to leave her car with the mechanic.
6. However long it takes, I'll stay until the end.
7. She insists she didn't take the money, but that's hard to believe.
8. Mark always works in the biology lab with Rita.
9. Linda plans to enroll in law school next semester.
10. I'm glad I taped the lecture, because I didn't understand a single word.
11. Denise was told to finish the last of the math problems.
12. In the storage closet she found several missing cartons of books.
13. That couldn't be all she said!
14. Alice made the salesman refund her money.
15. Only Eric can play the piano so well.
16. He should plan on working at least two hours on that outline.
17. Mr. Milton was appointed dean of the college last year.

18. The place to find out about part-time jobs is the employment office.
19. To think that he would lie to you.
20. If you are going to move out of your apartment, you should give the landlord thirty days' notice.

Part B

Directions: In Part B you will hear short conversations between two speakers. At the end of each conversation, a third person will ask a question about what was said. You will hear each conversation and question about it just one time. Therefore, you must listen carefully to understand what each speaker says. After you hear a conversation and the question about it, read the four possible answers in your test book and decide which one is the best answer to the question you heard. Then, on your answer sheet, find the number of the question and fill in the space that corresponds to the letter of the answer you have chosen.

Look at the following example.

You will hear:
    Man: That exam was just awful.
  Woman: Oh, it could have been worse.
      Q: What does the woman mean?

You will read:
  (A) The exam was really awful.
  (B) It was the worst exam she had ever seen.
  (C) It couldn't have been more difficult.
  (D) It was not that hard.

From the conversation you learn that the man thought the exam was very difficult and that the woman disagreed with the man. The best answer to the question "What does the woman mean?" is (D), "It wasn't that hard." Therefore, you should choose answer (D).

21.   **Man:** I'd like two tickets to Vancouver.
  Woman: You'd better hurry. The flight takes off in just a few minutes.
    Q: Where does this conversation probably take place?

22.   **Man:** Did you buy the perfume that you liked so much?
  Woman: Unfortunately, I only had ten dollars with me.
    Q: What does the woman suggest?

23. **Woman:** Why don't you water the plants, Mark?
  Man: But I watered them yesterday.
    Q: What does Mark mean?

24. **Woman:** Do you think Paul will come play tennis with us this afternoon?
  Man: I believe he's out of town.
    Q: What does the man imply about Paul?

25.   **Man:** Did it cost very much to stay overnight at the hotel?
  Woman: More than you would believe.
    Q: What does the woman mean?

26. **Woman:** The checks aren't in my purse.
  Man: Why don't you look in your suitcase?
    Q: What does the man mean?

27. **Woman:** Eric twisted his ankle playing basketball.
  Man: Can he walk on it?
    Q: What does the man want to know?

28.   **Man:** Should I get the plaid shirt or the striped one?
  Woman: It's all the same to me.
    Q: What does the woman mean?

29.   **Man:** The car won't start. Maybe I should call a service station.
  Woman: Did you check to see if there's any gas?
    Q: What does the woman want to know?

30. **Woman:** That was sure a loud meeting.
  Man: Everyone seemed to have something to say.
    Q: What did they imply about the meeting?

31. **Woman:** We are unable to accept your housing application because it's well past the deadline.
  Man: But what am I supposed to do about housing?
    Q: What does the man imply?

32. **Man:** Have you been working on your biology homework?
   Woman: What homework is that?
   Q: Why is the woman surprised?

33. **Man:** I can't believe that you made that bracelet.
   Woman: It's really not too hard. It just takes a lot of time.
   Q: What is the woman saying about the bracelet?

34. **Woman:** Have you read the article Stan wrote for the school paper?
   Man: Read it? I typed it for him.
   Q: What does the man mean?

35. **Man:** Did Bob get the promotion he wanted?
   Woman: Yes, and he's really ecstatic.
   Q: What is the woman saying about Bob?

Part C

Directions: In this part of the test, you will hear short talks and conversations. After each of them, you will be asked some questions. You will hear the talks and conversations and the questions about them just one time. They will not be written out for you. Therefore, you must listen carefully to understand what each speaker says.

After you hear a question, read the four possible answers in your test book and decide which one is the best answer to the question you heard. Then, on your answer sheet, find the number of the question and fill in the space that corresponds to the letter of the answer you have chosen.

Listen to this sample talk.

You will hear:
   Artist Grant Wood was a guiding force in the school of painting known as American regionalist, a style reflecting the distinctive characteristics of art from rural areas of the United States. Wood began drawing animals on the family farm at the age of three, and when he was thirty-eight one of his paintings received a remarkable amount of public notice and acclaim. This painting, called *American Gothic*, is a starkly simple depiction of a serious couple staring directly out at the viewer.

Now look at the following example.

You will hear:
   What style of painting is known as American regionalist?

You will read:
   (A) Art from America's inner cities.
   (B) Art from the central region of the U.S.
   (C) Art from various urban areas in the U.S.
   (D) Art from rural sections of America.

The best answer to the question "What style of painting is known as American regionalist?" is (D), "Art from rural sections of America." Therefore, you should choose answer (D).

Now look at the next example.

You will hear:
   What is the name of Wood's most successful painting?

You will read:
   (A) *American Regionalist.*
   (B) *The Family Farm in Iowa.*
   (C) *American Gothic.*
   (D) *A Serious Couple.*

The best answer to the question "What is the name of Wood's most successful painting?" is (C), *"American Gothic."* Therefore, you should choose answer (C).

Questions 36 through 40 are based on the following conversation.

Woman: Hi, Mike. I've been trying to get in touch with you. I wanted to ask you about the Introduction to Sociology course you took last semester with Professor Patterson.
Man: Why did you want to know about that course?
Woman: Well, Professor Patterson is teaching it again next semester, and I think I might take it.
Man: I wouldn't do that if I were you.
Woman: Why not? Was it a terrible course?
Man: All the professor did was lecture day after day after day. He's a good enough lecturer, but I prefer courses where the students can participate more. I found it quite boring.

Woman: That course doesn't sound so bad to me. In fact, I like that kind of course. You can listen to the professor's ideas and not feel any pressure to come up with something to say.

Man: Well then maybe this course is for you.

36. Who is taking part in this conversation?
37. Why does the woman want to talk with Mike?
38. What type of class are they talking about?
39. What kind of course does the man prefer?
40. How does the woman feel about Professor Patterson's course?

Questions 41 through 45 are based on the following talk.

The California Gold Rush, which figured so prominently in the development of the West, was actually the result of a chance happening. Captain John Sutter received the rights to a large piece of land near what is today Sacramento, in northern California. Sutter's main purpose was to develop a lumber business from the huge expanses of trees on his property. It was during the construction of a sawmill for his lumber business that gold was found on the bank of the American River. As news about the gold spread, thousands of gold prospectors descended on Sutter's property. Sutter's business was destroyed by the prospectors and Sutter received little from the gold that was found there. Although Sutter died a poor and disheartened man, the population of California increased tremendously because of what was found on his property.

41. In which course would this lecture probably be given?
42. What kind of business was Sutter undertaking?
43. When was gold discovered on Sutter's farm?
44. What benefit did Sutter receive from the discovery of gold on his property?
45. What is the speaker's main point in this lecture?

Questions 46 through 50 are based on the following conversation.

Woman: Did you hear the story on the news this morning about the apartment fire down the street?

Man: I heard something about it. What happened exactly?

Woman: A fire started about 3 o'clock in the morning in an apartment complex with about twenty apartments. One of the apartments was completely destroyed, and several of the others were damaged.

Man: Do they know how the fire started?

Woman: They're not sure at this point, but they believe that it was started by someone smoking in bed. It's a shame that one careless person can cause so much trauma for others, not to mention the thousands and thousands of dollars of damage.

Man: Even more serious than the damage to property is the harm to the apartment's occupants. I hear that several residents were rushed to the hospital, but at least none of them died.

Woman: It's all so frightening. Do you know of anything I can do to keep this from happening to me?

Man: I guess the best thing to protect yourself is to make sure that you have a smoke alarm and a fire extinguisher in good working condition. The smoke alarm will give you an early warning that a fire has started, so you can call the fire department. If it is a small fire, maybe you can use the fire extinguisher to help put out the fire before the fire trucks arrive.

Woman: That's good advice. I think I'll go home and check my smoke alarm.

46. What is the topic of this conversation?
47. According to the woman, how extensively were the apartments damaged?
48. What did the man say about some of the apartment residents?
49. What advice does the man give to the woman to protect herself from fires?
50. According to the man, what is the purpose of a smoke alarm?

PRACTICE TEST FIVE TAPESCRIPT

SECTION 1
LISTENING COMPREHENSION

In this section of the test, you will have an opportunity to demonstrate your ability to understand spoken English. There are three parts in this section, with special directions for each part.

Part A

Directions: For each question in Part A, you will hear a short sentence. Each sentence will be spoken just one time. The sentences you hear will not be written out for you. Therefore, you must listen carefully to understand what the speaker says.

After you hear a sentence, read the four choices in your test book, marked (A), (B), (C), and (D), and decide which one is closest in meaning to the sentence you heard. Then, on your answer sheet, find the number of the question and fill in the space that corresponds to the letter of the answer you have chosen. Fill in the space so the letter inside the oval cannot be seen.

Example I

You will hear:
    John was the fastest runner in the race.

You will read:
(A) John outran the others.
(B) John was the fastest hunter in the chase.
(C) John wasn't the slowest in the race.
(D) John was the last runner to finish the race.

The speaker said, "John was the fastest runner in the race." Sentence (A), "John outran the others," is closest in meaning to the sentence you heard. Therefore, you should choose answer (A).

Example II

You will hear:
    Could you help me move my desk?

You will read:
(A) Could you help me use the rest?
(B) Do you mind using the other desk?
(C) Would you mind helping me carry this piece of furniture?
(D) If you move my desk, I'll help you with your work.

The speaker said, "Could you help me move my desk?" Sentence (C), "Would you mind helping me carry this piece of furniture?" is closest in meaning to the sentence you heard. Therefore, you should choose answer (C).

1. Alice graduated from journalism school, and so did Joe.
2. I'll take care of the bill.
3. It's fairly easy for students to find apartments near the university.
4. The seminar was quite boring, wasn't it?
5. Your laundry needs to be done tonight.
6. Do you want to walk on the beach after dinner?
7. It was so hot today that I couldn't get much work done.
8. He was elected president of the student council.
9. It's important to have insurance for your car.
10. When can you be ready to leave?
11. Adam has one brother and one sister, both younger.
12. Only once has a larger crowd attended a football game.
13. Steve's annoyed about the grade he received in economics.

14. The class meets twice a week, for an hour and a half each time.

15. I didn't expect to find you here when I returned.

16. The boys played football and then had some ice cream.

17. Gary, I hope that you'll be able to get on the next flight.

18. Without question, you need to improve the quality of your writing.

19. Although she's received many good reviews, she's not very famous.

20. I probably left the file of letters in my office.

Part B

Directions: In Part B you will hear short conversations between two speakers. At the end of each conversation, a third person will ask a question about what was said. You will hear each conversation and question about it just one time. Therefore, you must listen carefully to understand what each speaker says. After you hear a conversation and the question about it, read the four possible answers in your test book and decide which one is the best answer to the question you heard. Then, on your answer sheet, find the number of the question and fill in the space that corresponds to the letter of the answer you have chosen.

Look at the following example.

You will hear:
  Man: That exam was just awful.
  Woman: Oh, it could have been worse.
  Q: What does the woman mean?

You will read:
  (A) The exam was really awful.
  (B) It was the worst exam she had ever seen.
  (C) It couldn't have been more difficult.
  (D) It wasn't that hard.

From the conversation you learn that the man thought the exam was very difficult and that the woman disagreed with the man. The best answer to the question "What does the woman mean?" is (D), "It wasn't that hard." Therefore, you should choose answer (D).

21. Woman: Are you skiing this afternoon?
    Man: I doubt it. The weather forecast is pretty bad.
    Q: What does the man mean?

22. Man: Did you spend a lot of money at the fair?
    Woman: Only every cent in my purse.
    Q: What does the woman mean?

23. Man: Can I still check out these books?
    Woman: Yes, the circulation desk doesn't close for an hour.
    Q: Where does this conversation probably take place?

24. Woman: Do you think I should sit in on the psychology class tomorrow?
    Man: Definitely, provided you read the chapter first.
    Q: What does the man suggest?

25. Man: I'm not really pleased with the way my clothes look.
    Woman: Maybe you should find another laundry.
    Q: What does the woman suggest?

26. Man: Have you heard about Tim? He had to rush to the emergency room.
    Woman: Really? I hope it's not too serious.
    Q: What does the woman imply?

27. Woman: Going home already?
    Man: Yes. It's late.
    Q: What does the man mean?

28. Woman: My doctor's told me to take these pills every day.
    Man: Isn't that a lot of medicine?
    Q: What does the man mean?

29. Man: Did you know there was a tornado yesterday?
    Woman: I saw it from my window.
    Q: What happened to the woman?

30. Man: Shouldn't you pack a sweater for your trip?
    Woman: I don't think so, as Hawaii should be quite warm.
    Q: What is the man concerned about?

31.   **Man:** Has George been preparing for his comprehensive exams?
    Woman: He's been moving at a turtle's pace.
    Q: What does the woman imply about George?

32.   **Woman:** The new printer should arrive in the computer lab soon.
    Man: They've been saying that for weeks now.
    Q: What does the man mean?

33.   **Woman:** Can I call you back in a few minutes?
    Man: Don't bother. I'll talk to you tomorrow.
    Q: What does the man imply?

34.   **Woman:** What do you think of the annual report?
    Man: I've seen better.
    Q: What does the man mean?

35.   **Woman:** Would you like to go to the opera tonight?
    Man: I'd prefer a trip to the dentist.
    Q: What does the man imply?

Part C

Directions: In this part of the test, you will hear short talks and conversations. After each of them, you will be asked some questions. You will hear the talks and conversations and the questions about them just one time. They will not be written out for you. Therefore, you must listen carefully to understand what each speaker says.

After you hear a question, read the four possible answers in your test book and decide which one is the best answer to the question you heard. Then, on your answer sheet, find the number of the question and fill in the space that corresponds to the letter of the answer you have chosen.

Listen to this sample talk.

You will hear:
    Artist Grant Wood was a guiding force in the school of painting known as American regionalist, a style reflecting the distinctive characteristics of art from rural areas of the United States. Wood began drawing animals on the family farm at the age of three, and when he was thirty-eight one of his paintings received a remarkable amount of public notice and acclaim. This painting, called *American Gothic*, is a starkly simple depiction of a serious couple staring directly out at the viewer.

Now look at the following example.

You will hear:
    What style of painting is known as American regionalist?

You will read:
    (A) Art from America's inner cities.
    (B) Art from the central region of the U.S.
    (C) Art from various urban areas in the U.S.
    (D) Art from rural sections of America.

The best answer to the question "What style of painting is known as American regionalist?" is (D), "Art from rural sections of America." Therefore, you should choose answer (D).

Now look at the next example.

You will hear:
    What is the name of Wood's most successful painting?

You will read:
    (A) *American Regionalist.*
    (B) *The Family Farm in Iowa.*
    (C) *American Gothic.*
    (D) *A Serious Couple.*

The best answer to the question "What is the name of Wood's most successful painting?" is (C), "*American Gothic.*" Therefore, you should choose answer (C).

Questions 36 through 40 are based on the following talk:

    Hello and welcome to campus. This morning there will be a short tour of the university before we head to the Administration Complex for registration. I've been selected to be your tour guide because I've been a student on this campus for three years, and I know my way around well.
    The first stop on our tour is the library. As you can see, it's a large library, with over 100,000 volumes. Additionally there are

journals, newspapers, and magazines from around the world. The library's open seven days a week from 8:00 A.M. to midnight.

From the library, we'll move on to the Student Center. In the Student Center you'll find the university bookstore, where you can purchase all the texts for the courses you're taking. You can also find a post office, a bank, a theater, a coffee shop, a travel agency, and a bowling alley in the Student Center. The Student Center's here to provide services and entertainment for the student body.

The final stop on our tour is the Administration Complex. In this area, you'll find the offices of university administrators and the Student Records office. The auditorium where registration takes place is also in the Administration Complex. Now that we have reached the Administration Complex, the next item on your agenda is registration. Good luck.

36. Who is the speaker?
37. What is the main topic of the talk?
38. What does the speaker suggest about the library?
39. According to the speaker, what is the purpose of the Student Center?
40. Where will registration take place?

Questions 41 through 45 are based on the following conversation.

Woman: I'm going to my health club this afternoon. Would you like to come along? You could try it out and see if you want to take out a membership.

Man: You belong to a health club? It seems that everyone I meet here is involved in some kind of exercise program!

Woman: Oh, exercise is very popular nowadays, and this health club's the best in the area. Why don't you try it today?

Man: I would like to get a little more exercise, but I'm not sure if a health club's the way to go.

Woman: This club has all kinds of exercise machines and classes, a track, racketball courts, and a sauna. It has every kind of exercise you could want, except perhaps a swimming pool.

Man: Well, I guess it can't hurt to try it just once. What time should we go?

41. Where is the woman going this afternoon?
42. Why does the woman ask the man to go?
43. Why is the man unsure about going?
44. According to the woman, what kinds of services does the health club offer?
45. What does the man decide to do?

Questions 46 through 50 are based on the following talk.

A major cause of water pollution in the 1950's was the use of synthetic detergents. Unlike natural soaps, which were biodegradable, synthetic detergents would not break down into simpler substances. When released into the water supply, these non-biodegradable synthetic detergents caused masses of foam to remain in both surface water and ground water.

In the 1960's new biodegradable detergents came into use, and the problem of foaming in lakes, rivers, and streams began to disappear. However, these new biodegradable detergents contained phosphates, and those phosphates presented an entirely different set of problems in maintaining a clean water supply.

46. What major cause of water pollution in the 1950's was presented in this talk?
47. What are biodegradable substances?
48. What happened when non-biodegradable synthetic detergents were released into the water supply?
49. What happened with detergents in the 1960's?
50. What will probably be the topic of the talk that follows?

ANSWERS TO PRACTICE TEST ONE

Section I: Listening Comprehension

1.	C	14.	A	27.	D	40.	D
2.	D	15.	D	28.	B	41.	A
3.	D	16.	B	29.	C	42.	C
4.	A	17.	A	30.	A	43.	C
5.	B	18.	B	31.	D	44.	C
6.	C	19.	D	32.	D	45.	D
7.	A	20.	A	33.	A	46.	B
8.	A	21.	A	34.	B	47.	D
9.	B	22.	C	35.	D	48.	B
10.	B	23.	C	36.	B	49.	A
11.	D	24.	D	37.	D	50.	C
12.	B	25.	C	38.	C		
13.	C	26.	B	39.	A		

Section II: Structure and Written Expression

1.	D	11.	A	21.	D	31.	C
2.	B	12.	A	22.	A	32.	A
3.	A	13.	C	23.	C	33.	A
4.	B	14.	C	24.	A	34.	B
5.	A	15.	D	25.	B	35.	A
6.	D	16.	D	26.	D	36.	A
7.	A	17.	C	27.	B	37.	C
8.	B	18.	D	28.	C	38.	D
9.	B	19.	A	29.	C	39.	B
10.	C	20.	D	30.	C	40.	A

Section III: Vocabulary and Reading

1.	B	16.	D	31.	C	46.	D
2.	A	17.	A	32.	D	47.	A
3.	C	18.	D	33.	B	48.	C
4.	A	19.	B	34.	D	49.	D
5.	D	20.	A	35.	B	50.	B
6.	B	21.	C	36.	B	51.	A
7.	C	22.	D	37.	A	52.	B
8.	B	23.	C	38.	D	53.	C
9.	D	24.	B	39.	C	54.	A
10.	A	25.	A	40.	B	55.	C
11.	A	26.	A	41.	D	56.	D
12.	B	27.	D	42.	C	57.	C
13.	C	28.	D	43.	A	58.	D
14.	C	29.	A	44.	B	59.	A
15.	C	30.	C	45.	D	60.	C

ANSWERS TO PRACTICE TEST TWO

Section I: Listening Comprehension

1.	D	14.	A	27.	A	40.	A
2.	A	15.	D	28.	B	41.	D
3.	C	16.	B	29.	D	42.	A
4.	B	17.	C	30.	A	43.	C
5.	C	18.	C	31.	D	44.	D
6.	A	19.	D	32.	C	45.	B
7.	D	20.	B	33.	B	46.	B
8.	B	21.	C	34.	B	47.	B
9.	A	22.	D	35.	C	48.	D
10.	C	23.	A	36.	C	49.	C
11.	B	24.	C	37.	D	50.	A
12.	C	25.	B	38.	C		
13.	D	26.	B	39.	B		

Section II: Structure and Written Expression

1.	D	11.	A	21.	B	31.	C
2.	B	12.	B	22.	B	32.	D
3.	D	13.	C	23.	A	33.	B
4.	B	14.	D	24.	A	34.	D
5.	A	15.	C	25.	B	35.	C
6.	C	16.	C	26.	A	36.	B
7.	D	17.	B	27.	C	37.	D
8.	B	18.	D	28.	D	38.	D
9.	C	19.	B	29.	C	39.	C
10.	A	20.	C	30.	A	40.	B

Section III: Vocabulary and Reading

1.	A	16.	A	31.	C	46.	A
2.	D	17.	B	32.	D	47.	B
3.	C	18.	B	33.	A	48.	D
4.	B	19.	D	34.	B	49.	C
5.	C	20.	D	35.	D	50.	C
6.	A	21.	C	36.	B	51.	A
7.	B	22.	B	37.	A	52.	B
8.	B	23.	A	38.	A	53.	C
9.	A	24.	D	39.	C	54.	D
10.	D	25.	C	40.	D	55.	C
11.	C	26.	A	41.	C	56.	C
12.	C	27.	A	42.	B	57.	D
13.	B	28.	B	43.	A	58.	A
14.	A	29.	D	44.	D	59.	A
15.	D	30.	A	45.	B	60.	B

ANSWERS TO PRACTICE TEST THREE

Section I: Listening Comprehension

1.	C	14.	C	27.	D	40.	C
2.	A	15.	D	28.	A	41.	B
3.	B	16.	D	29.	D	42.	D
4.	D	17.	A	30.	B	43.	C
5.	C	18.	A	31.	D	44.	D
6.	B	19.	B	32.	A	45.	B
7.	A	20.	C	33.	A	46.	D
8.	D	21.	C	34.	B	47.	B
9.	C	22.	B	35.	C	48.	D
10.	D	23.	D	36.	B	49.	B
11.	C	24.	C	37.	C	50.	A
12.	C	25.	D	38.	D		
13.	A	26.	A	39.	A		

Section II: Structure and Written Expression

1.	A	11.	A	21.	C	31.	C
2.	C	12.	B	22.	A	32.	D
3.	B	13.	D	23.	B	33.	D
4.	C	14.	C	24.	D	34.	A
5.	A	15.	D	25.	A	35.	A
6.	D	16.	A	26.	D	36.	A
7.	B	17.	B	27.	B	37.	D
8.	C	18.	D	28.	C	38.	A
9.	B	19.	A	29.	B	39.	D
10.	A	20.	C	30.	A	40.	A

Section III: Vocabulary and Reading

1.	B	16.	C	31.	B	46.	D
2.	C	17.	A	32.	A	47.	C
3.	A	18.	C	33.	C	48.	C
4.	B	19.	C	34.	D	49.	D
5.	A	20.	D	35.	D	50.	A
6.	D	21.	B	36.	D	51.	B
7.	A	22.	A	37.	A	52.	C
8.	B	23.	C	38.	B	53.	D
9.	C	24.	D	39.	D	54.	B
10.	C	25.	C	40.	C	55.	A
11.	A	26.	B	41.	B	56.	C
12.	A	27.	B	42.	C	57.	B
13.	D	28.	D	43.	B	58.	D
14.	B	29.	A	44.	D	59.	A
15.	C	30.	B	45.	A	60.	C

ANSWERS TO PRACTICE TEST FOUR

Section I: Listening Comprehension

1.	C	14.	D	27.	C	40.	C
2.	B	.15.	A	28.	B	41.	C
3.	D	16.	B	29.	A	42.	B
4.	D	17.	D	30.	D	43.	A
5.	A	18.	B	31.	C	44.	D
6.	B	19.	A	32.	B	45.	D
7.	C	20.	C	33.	B	46.	C
8.	A	21.	C	34.	C	47.	A
9.	D	22.	D	35.	D	48.	B
10.	C	23.	B	36.	A	49.	D
11.	B	24.	B	37.	C	50.	B
12.	C	25.	D	38.	B		
13.	D	26.	A	39.	D		

Section II: Structure and Written Expression

1.	B	11.	A	21.	C	31.	C
2.	B	12.	B	22.	D	32.	A
3.	D	13.	D	23.	D	33.	D
4.	A	14.	A	24.	B	34.	B
5.	C	15.	C	25.	D	35.	D
6.	A	16.	D	26.	D	36.	B
7.	C	17.	C	27.	C	37.	D
8.	D	18.	A	28.	C	38.	D
9.	C	19.	D	29.	C	39.	A
10.	C	20.	B	30.	C	40.	D

Section III: Vocabulary and Reading

1.	A	16.	C	31.	A	46.	C
2.	A	17.	D	32.	B	47.	B
3.	B	18.	C	33.	D	48.	A
4.	C	19.	A	34.	D	49.	A
5.	B	20.	D	35.	C	50.	D
6.	C	21.	D	36.	D	51.	B
7.	D	22.	B	37.	C	52.	D
8.	A	23.	A	38.	D	53.	C
9.	D	24.	B	39.	B	54.	B
10.	B	25.	A	40.	C	55.	D
11.	C	26.	C	41.	A	56.	B
12.	C	27.	B	42.	B	57.	C
13.	B	28.	C	43.	D	58.	D
14.	A	29.	D	44.	C	59.	D
15.	B	30.	A	45.	B	60.	A

ANSWERS TO PRACTICE TEST FIVE

Section I: Listening Comprehension

1.	A	14.	B	27.	A	40.	C
2.	C	15.	D	28.	C	41.	B
3.	B	16.	D	29.	B	42.	C
4.	D	17.	A	30.	C	43.	C
5.	D	18.	B	31.	D	44.	D
6.	A	19.	C	32.	A	45.	A
7.	B	20.	C	33.	D	46.	B
8.	C	21.	B	34.	D	47.	C
9.	C	22.	C	35.	B	48.	B
10.	D	23.	A	36.	B	49.	D
11.	C	24.	D	37.	D	50.	D
12.	A	25.	B	38.	C		
13.	C	26.	D	39.	A		

Section II: Structure and Written Expression

1.	A	11.	C	21.	D	31.	A
2.	B	12.	B	22.	B	32.	C
3.	C	13.	C	23.	A	33.	C
4.	B	14.	D	24.	D	34.	B
5.	D	15.	B	25.	A	35.	D
6.	A	16.	D	26.	A	36.	A
7.	C	17.	A	27.	D	37.	A
8.	C	18.	D	28.	D	38.	D
9.	A	19.	A	29.	A	39.	C
10.	C	20.	B	30.	D	40.	C

Section III: Vocabulary and Reading

1.	D	16.	A	31.	D	46.	C
2.	D	17.	A	32.	A	47.	D
3.	A	18.	D	33.	B	48.	C
4.	B	19.	B	34.	B	49.	A
5.	B	20.	C	35.	D	50.	C
6.	D	21.	B	36.	C	51.	C
7.	A	22.	A	37.	C	52.	A
8.	B	23.	D	38.	B	53.	D
9.	C	24.	B	39.	D	54.	D
10.	B	25.	D	40.	A	55.	C
11.	B	26.	A	41.	B	56.	A
12.	B	27.	C	42.	C	57.	D
13.	D	28.	D	43.	A	58.	C
14.	A	29.	B	44.	D	59.	C
15.	B	30.	D	45.	B	60.	B

SCORING YOUR PRACTICE TESTS

When your TOEFL is scored, you will receive a score between 20 and 70 in each of the three sections (Listening, Structure and Written Expression, Vocabulary and Reading). You will also receive an overall score between 200 and 700. You can use the following chart to estimate the scores on your TOEFL practice tests.

NUMBER CORRECT	CONVERTED SCORE SECTION 1	CONVERTED SCORE SECTION 2	CONVERTED SCORE SECTION 3
60	—	—	67
59	—	—	66
58	—	—	65
57	—	—	64
56	—	—	63
55	—	—	62
54	—	—	61
53	—	—	61
52	—	—	60
51	—	—	59
50	68	—	58
49	66	—	58
48	64	—	57
47	63	—	56
46	62	—	56
45	61	—	55
44	60	—	54
43	59	—	54
42	58	—	53
41	57	—	52
40	57	68	52
39	56	65	51
38	55	64	50
37	54	63	50
36	53	61	49
35	53	59	48
34	52	58	48
33	51	57	47
32	51	56	47
31	50	54	46
30	49	53	45
29	49	52	45
28	48	51	44
27	48	50	43
26	47	49	43
25	47	48	42
24	46	47	41

NUMBER CORRECT	CONVERTED SCORE SECTION 1	CONVERTED SCORE SECTION 2	CONVERTED SCORE SECTION 3
23	45	46	40
22	45	45	40
21	44	44	39
20	43	43	38
19	43	42	37
18	42	41	36
17	42	40	35
16	41	39	34
15	40	38	33
14	39	37	32
13	38	36	31
12	37	35	30
11	36	34	29
10	35	34	28
9	33	33	27
8	32	31	26
7	31	30	26
6	30	28	25
5	29	26	24
4	28	25	24
3	27	24	23
2	25	23	22
1	22	21	21
0	20	20	20

You should first use the chart to determine your converted score for each section. Suppose that you got 30 correct in the first section, 28 correct in the second section, and 43 correct in the third section. The 30 correct in the first section means a converted score of 49. The 28 correct in the second section means a converted score of 51. The 43 correct in the third section means a converted score of 54.

	SECTION 1	SECTION 2	SECTION 3
NUMBER CORRECT	30	28	43
CONVERTED SCORE	49	51	54

Next you should determine your overall score in the following way:

1. Add the three converted scores together.

   $$49 + 51 + 54 = 154$$

2. Divide the sum by 3.

   $$154/3 = 51.3$$

3. Then multiply by 10.

   $$51.3 \times 10 = 513$$

The overall TOEFL score in this example is 513.

SCORING YOUR PRACTICE TESTS

The score of the TWE is included on the same form as your regular TOEFL score, but it is not part of your overall TOEFL score. It is a separate score on a scale of 1 to 6, where 1 is the worst score and 6 is the best score. The following table outlines what each of the scores essentially means:

TEST OF WRITTEN ENGLISH SCORES

6	The writer has very strong organizational, structural, and grammatical skills.
5	The writer has good organizational, structural, and grammatical skills. However, the essay contains some errors.
4	The writer has adequate organizational, structural, and grammatical skills. The essay contains a number of errors.
3	The writer shows evidence of organizational, structural, and grammatical skills that still need to be improved.
2	The writer shows a minimal ability to convey ideas in written English.
1	The writer is not capable of conveying ideas in written English.

CHARTING YOUR PROGRESS

Each time you take a practice test, you should record the results in the chart that follows. In this way you will be able to keep track of the progress you make. You will also be aware of the areas of the TOEFL that you still need to improve.

	LISTENING COMPREHENSION	STRUCTURE AND WRITTEN EXPRESSION	VOCABULARY AND READING	OVERALL SCORE
TEST 1				
TEST 2				
TEST 3				
TEST 4				
TEST 5				

TEST OF ENGLISH AS A FOREIGN LANGUAGE

SIDE 1

THIS IS A SAMPLE ANSWER SHEET

Use a No. 2 (H.B.) pencil only. Do not use ink. Be sure each mark is dark and completely fills the intended oval. Erase errors or stray marks completely.

1. NAME: Print your name as it appears on your admission ticket, first print your family name (surname), then your given name, and then your middle name. Leave one box blank between names. Then, below each box, fill in the oval that contains the same letter.

2. REGISTRATION NUMBER

→ Start here

YOUR REGISTRATION NUMBER IS PRINTED TO THE RIGHT AND IS IN MACHINE READABLE FORM.

DO NOT RE-ENTER THE NUMBER HERE.

3. INSTITUTION AND DEPARTMENT CODES: Give the code numbers of the institutions and departments to which you want your official score report sent. Be sure to fill in the corresponding oval below each box.

INSTITUTION CODE / DEPT CODE

4. DO YOU PLAN TO STUDY FOR A DEGREE IN THE U.S.A. OR CANADA?

○ YES   ○ NO

5. REASON FOR TAKING TOEFL (FILL IN ONLY ONE OVAL)

1. To enter a college or university as an undergraduate student.
2. To enter a college or university as a graduate student.
3. To enter a school other than a college or university.
4. To become licensed to practice my profession in the U.S.A. or Canada.
5. To demonstrate my proficiency in English to the company for which I work or expect to work.
6. Other than the above (please specify)

6. NUMBER OF TIMES YOU HAVE TAKEN TOEFL BEFORE

○ NONE   ○ ONE   ○ TWO   ○ THREE   ○ FOUR OR MORE

7. CENTER (Print.)

COUNTRY / CITY / CENTER NUMBER

8. PLEASE PRINT IN BLOCK LETTERS YOUR NAME AND MAILING ADDRESS.

FAMILY NAME (SURNAME) / GIVEN (FIRST) NAME / MIDDLE NAME

STREET ADDRESS OR P.O. BOX NO

CITY / STATE OR PROVINCE

POSTAL OR ZIP CODE / COUNTRY

9. SIGNATURE AND DATE: Please copy the following statement in the space provided below; use handwriting.

"I hereby agree to the conditions set forth in the Bulletin of Information and affirm that I am the person whose name and address are given on this answer sheet."

Also sign your name on the line provided and enter today's date (in numbers).

SIGNED: _____ (WRITE YOUR NAME AS IF SIGNING A BUSINESS LETTER)

DATE: ___ MO / DAY / YEAR

DO NOT WRITE IN THIS AREA.

0   2   1   5   2   3   5

DO NOT MARK IN THIS AREA.

TEST FORM:

FORM

TEST BOOK SERIAL NUMBER

SEAT NUMBER

SEX	DATE OF BIRTH
☐ MALE ☐ FEMALE	MO / DAY / YEAR

Choose only one answer for each question. Carefully and completely fill in the oval corresponding to the answer you choose so that the letter inside the oval cannot be seen. Completely erase any other marks you may have made. Choose only one answer for each question.

CORRECT	WRONG	WRONG	WRONG	WRONG
Ⓐ Ⓑ ● Ⓓ	Ⓐ Ⓑ ⊗ Ⓓ	Ⓐ Ⓑ ✗ Ⓓ	Ⓐ Ⓑ ⊖ Ⓓ	Ⓐ Ⓑ ◉ Ⓓ

NAME (Print) _____

FAMILY NAME (SURNAME)　　　　　GIVEN (FIRST NAME)　　　　　MIDDLE NAME

REGISTRATION NUMBER　　　**SIGNATURE**

Reproduced by permission.

THIS IS A SAMPLE ONLY

SECTION 1

1 Ⓐ Ⓑ Ⓒ Ⓓ
2 Ⓐ Ⓑ Ⓒ Ⓓ
3 Ⓐ Ⓑ Ⓒ Ⓓ
4 Ⓐ Ⓑ Ⓒ Ⓓ
5 Ⓐ Ⓑ Ⓒ Ⓓ
6 Ⓐ Ⓑ Ⓒ Ⓓ
7 Ⓐ Ⓑ Ⓒ Ⓓ
8 Ⓐ Ⓑ Ⓒ Ⓓ
9 Ⓐ Ⓑ Ⓒ Ⓓ
10 Ⓐ Ⓑ Ⓒ Ⓓ
11 Ⓐ Ⓑ Ⓒ Ⓓ
12 Ⓐ Ⓑ Ⓒ Ⓓ
13 Ⓐ Ⓑ Ⓒ Ⓓ
14 Ⓐ Ⓑ Ⓒ Ⓓ
15 Ⓐ Ⓑ Ⓒ Ⓓ
16 Ⓐ Ⓑ Ⓒ Ⓓ
17 Ⓐ Ⓑ Ⓒ Ⓓ
18 Ⓐ Ⓑ Ⓒ Ⓓ
19 Ⓐ Ⓑ Ⓒ Ⓓ
20 Ⓐ Ⓑ Ⓒ Ⓓ
21 Ⓐ Ⓑ Ⓒ Ⓓ
22 Ⓐ Ⓑ Ⓒ Ⓓ
23 Ⓐ Ⓑ Ⓒ Ⓓ
24 Ⓐ Ⓑ Ⓒ Ⓓ
25 Ⓐ Ⓑ Ⓒ Ⓓ
26 Ⓐ Ⓑ Ⓒ Ⓓ
27 Ⓐ Ⓑ Ⓒ Ⓓ
28 Ⓐ Ⓑ Ⓒ Ⓓ
29 Ⓐ Ⓑ Ⓒ Ⓓ
30 Ⓐ Ⓑ Ⓒ Ⓓ
31 Ⓐ Ⓑ Ⓒ Ⓓ
32 Ⓐ Ⓑ Ⓒ Ⓓ
33 Ⓐ Ⓑ Ⓒ Ⓓ
34 Ⓐ Ⓑ Ⓒ Ⓓ
35 Ⓐ Ⓑ Ⓒ Ⓓ
36 Ⓐ Ⓑ Ⓒ Ⓓ
37 Ⓐ Ⓑ Ⓒ Ⓓ
38 Ⓐ Ⓑ Ⓒ Ⓓ
39 Ⓐ Ⓑ Ⓒ Ⓓ
40 Ⓐ Ⓑ Ⓒ Ⓓ
41 Ⓐ Ⓑ Ⓒ Ⓓ
42 Ⓐ Ⓑ Ⓒ Ⓓ
43 Ⓐ Ⓑ Ⓒ Ⓓ
44 Ⓐ Ⓑ Ⓒ Ⓓ
45 Ⓐ Ⓑ Ⓒ Ⓓ
46 Ⓐ Ⓑ Ⓒ Ⓓ
47 Ⓐ Ⓑ Ⓒ Ⓓ
48 Ⓐ Ⓑ Ⓒ Ⓓ
49 Ⓐ Ⓑ Ⓒ Ⓓ
50 Ⓐ Ⓑ Ⓒ Ⓓ

SECTION 2

1 Ⓐ Ⓑ Ⓒ Ⓓ
2 Ⓐ Ⓑ Ⓒ Ⓓ
3 Ⓐ Ⓑ Ⓒ Ⓓ
4 Ⓐ Ⓑ Ⓒ Ⓓ
5 Ⓐ Ⓑ Ⓒ Ⓓ
6 Ⓐ Ⓑ Ⓒ Ⓓ
7 Ⓐ Ⓑ Ⓒ Ⓓ
8 Ⓐ Ⓑ Ⓒ Ⓓ
9 Ⓐ Ⓑ Ⓒ Ⓓ
10 Ⓐ Ⓑ Ⓒ Ⓓ
11 Ⓐ Ⓑ Ⓒ Ⓓ
12 Ⓐ Ⓑ Ⓒ Ⓓ
13 Ⓐ Ⓑ Ⓒ Ⓓ
14 Ⓐ Ⓑ Ⓒ Ⓓ
15 Ⓐ Ⓑ Ⓒ Ⓓ
16 Ⓐ Ⓑ Ⓒ Ⓓ
17 Ⓐ Ⓑ Ⓒ Ⓓ
18 Ⓐ Ⓑ Ⓒ Ⓓ
19 Ⓐ Ⓑ Ⓒ Ⓓ
20 Ⓐ Ⓑ Ⓒ Ⓓ
21 Ⓐ Ⓑ Ⓒ Ⓓ
22 Ⓐ Ⓑ Ⓒ Ⓓ
23 Ⓐ Ⓑ Ⓒ Ⓓ
24 Ⓐ Ⓑ Ⓒ Ⓓ
25 Ⓐ Ⓑ Ⓒ Ⓓ
26 Ⓐ Ⓑ Ⓒ Ⓓ
27 Ⓐ Ⓑ Ⓒ Ⓓ
28 Ⓐ Ⓑ Ⓒ Ⓓ
29 Ⓐ Ⓑ Ⓒ Ⓓ
30 Ⓐ Ⓑ Ⓒ Ⓓ
31 Ⓐ Ⓑ Ⓒ Ⓓ
32 Ⓐ Ⓑ Ⓒ Ⓓ
33 Ⓐ Ⓑ Ⓒ Ⓓ
34 Ⓐ Ⓑ Ⓒ Ⓓ
35 Ⓐ Ⓑ Ⓒ Ⓓ
36 Ⓐ Ⓑ Ⓒ Ⓓ
37 Ⓐ Ⓑ Ⓒ Ⓓ
38 Ⓐ Ⓑ Ⓒ Ⓓ
39 Ⓐ Ⓑ Ⓒ Ⓓ
40 Ⓐ Ⓑ Ⓒ Ⓓ

SECTION 3

1 Ⓐ Ⓑ Ⓒ Ⓓ　　31 Ⓐ Ⓑ Ⓒ Ⓓ
2 Ⓐ Ⓑ Ⓒ Ⓓ　　32 Ⓐ Ⓑ Ⓒ Ⓓ
3 Ⓐ Ⓑ Ⓒ Ⓓ　　33 Ⓐ Ⓑ Ⓒ Ⓓ
4 Ⓐ Ⓑ Ⓒ Ⓓ　　34 Ⓐ Ⓑ Ⓒ Ⓓ
5 Ⓐ Ⓑ Ⓒ Ⓓ　　35 Ⓐ Ⓑ Ⓒ Ⓓ
6 Ⓐ Ⓑ Ⓒ Ⓓ　　36 Ⓐ Ⓑ Ⓒ Ⓓ
7 Ⓐ Ⓑ Ⓒ Ⓓ　　37 Ⓐ Ⓑ Ⓒ Ⓓ
8 Ⓐ Ⓑ Ⓒ Ⓓ　　38 Ⓐ Ⓑ Ⓒ Ⓓ
9 Ⓐ Ⓑ Ⓒ Ⓓ　　39 Ⓐ Ⓑ Ⓒ Ⓓ
10 Ⓐ Ⓑ Ⓒ Ⓓ　　40 Ⓐ Ⓑ Ⓒ Ⓓ
11 Ⓐ Ⓑ Ⓒ Ⓓ　　41 Ⓐ Ⓑ Ⓒ Ⓓ
12 Ⓐ Ⓑ Ⓒ Ⓓ　　42 Ⓐ Ⓑ Ⓒ Ⓓ
13 Ⓐ Ⓑ Ⓒ Ⓓ　　43 Ⓐ Ⓑ Ⓒ Ⓓ
14 Ⓐ Ⓑ Ⓒ Ⓓ　　44 Ⓐ Ⓑ Ⓒ Ⓓ
15 Ⓐ Ⓑ Ⓒ Ⓓ　　45 Ⓐ Ⓑ Ⓒ Ⓓ
16 Ⓐ Ⓑ Ⓒ Ⓓ　　46 Ⓐ Ⓑ Ⓒ Ⓓ
17 Ⓐ Ⓑ Ⓒ Ⓓ　　47 Ⓐ Ⓑ Ⓒ Ⓓ
18 Ⓐ Ⓑ Ⓒ Ⓓ　　48 Ⓐ Ⓑ Ⓒ Ⓓ
19 Ⓐ Ⓑ Ⓒ Ⓓ　　49 Ⓐ Ⓑ Ⓒ Ⓓ
20 Ⓐ Ⓑ Ⓒ Ⓓ　　50 Ⓐ Ⓑ Ⓒ Ⓓ
21 Ⓐ Ⓑ Ⓒ Ⓓ　　51 Ⓐ Ⓑ Ⓒ Ⓓ
22 Ⓐ Ⓑ Ⓒ Ⓓ　　52 Ⓐ Ⓑ Ⓒ Ⓓ
23 Ⓐ Ⓑ Ⓒ Ⓓ　　53 Ⓐ Ⓑ Ⓒ Ⓓ
24 Ⓐ Ⓑ Ⓒ Ⓓ　　54 Ⓐ Ⓑ Ⓒ Ⓓ
25 Ⓐ Ⓑ Ⓒ Ⓓ　　55 Ⓐ Ⓑ Ⓒ Ⓓ
26 Ⓐ Ⓑ Ⓒ Ⓓ　　56 Ⓐ Ⓑ Ⓒ Ⓓ
27 Ⓐ Ⓑ Ⓒ Ⓓ　　57 Ⓐ Ⓑ Ⓒ Ⓓ
28 Ⓐ Ⓑ Ⓒ Ⓓ　　58 Ⓐ Ⓑ Ⓒ Ⓓ
29 Ⓐ Ⓑ Ⓒ Ⓓ　　59 Ⓐ Ⓑ Ⓒ Ⓓ
30 Ⓐ Ⓑ Ⓒ Ⓓ　　60 Ⓐ Ⓑ Ⓒ Ⓓ

SAMPLE

SCORE CANCELLATION

If you want to cancel your scores from this administration, complete A and B below. The scores will not be sent to you or your designated recipients, and they will be deleted from your permanent record. To cancel your scores from this test administration, you must:

A. fill in both ovals here　and B. sign your name in full below

○ — ○

ONCE A SCORE IS CANCELED, IT CANNOT BE REINSTATED ON YOUR PERMANENT RECORD.

1R	2R	3R	TCS	FOR ETS USE ONLY	F
1CS	2CS	3CS			

REGISTRATION NUMBER		TEST CENTER		TEST BOOK SERIAL NUMBER		TEST DATE

Begin your essay here. If you need more space, use the other side.

TOPIC

Q1381-07

DO NOT WRITE IN THIS AREA.

0   0   7   3   2   0   7

Reprinted by permission.

THIS IS A SAMPLE ANSWER SHEET

DO NOT WRITE BELOW THIS LINE. FOR ETS USE ONLY.

ORS

NO

OFF

TEST OF ENGLISH AS A FOREIGN LANGUAGE

SIDE 1

THIS IS A SAMPLE ANSWER SHEET

DO NOT WRITE IN THIS AREA.

0   2   1   5   2   3   5

1. NAME: Print your name as it appears on your admission ticket. Using one box for each letter, first print your family name (surname), then your given name, and then your middle name. Leave one box blank between names. Then, below each box, fill in the oval that contains the same letter.

Use a No. 2 (H.B.) pencil only. Do not use ink. Be sure each mark is dark and completely fills the intended oval. Erase errors or stray marks completely.

2. REGISTRATION NUMBER
→ Start here

YOUR
REGISTRATION
NUMBER IS
PRINTED TO
THE RIGHT
AND IS IN
MACHINE
READABLE
FORM.

DO NOT
RE-ENTER
THE NUMBER
HERE.

3. INSTITUTION AND DEPARTMENT CODES: Give the code numbers of the institutions and departments to which you want your official score report sent. Be sure to fill in the corresponding oval below each box.

INSTITUTION CODE | DEPT. CODE (repeated columns)

4. DO YOU PLAN TO STUDY FOR A DEGREE IN THE U.S.A. OR CANADA?

◯ YES   ◯ NO

5. REASON FOR TAKING TOEFL (FILL IN ONLY ONE OVAL.)

◯ 1. To enter a college or university as an undergraduate student.
◯ 2. To enter a college or university as a graduate student.
◯ 3. To enter a school other than a college or university.
◯ 4. To become licensed to practice my profession in the U.S.A. or Canada.
◯ 5. To demonstrate my proficiency in English to the company for which I work or expect to work.
◯ 6. Other than the above (please specify)

6. NUMBER OF TIMES YOU HAVE TAKEN TOEFL BEFORE?

◯ NONE   ◯ THREE
◯ ONE   ◯ FOUR OR MORE
◯ TWO

7. CENTER (Print).

CITY
COUNTRY
CENTER NUMBER

8. PLEASE PRINT IN BLOCK LETTERS YOUR NAME AND MAILING ADDRESS.

FAMILY NAME (SURNAME)   GIVEN (FIRST) NAME   MIDDLE NAME
STREET ADDRESS OR P.O. BOX NO.
CITY   STATE OR PROVINCE
POSTAL OR ZIP CODE   COUNTRY

9. SIGNATURE AND DATE: Please copy the following statement in the space provided below; use handwriting.

"I hereby agree to the conditions set forth in the Bulletin of Information and affirm that I am the person whose name and address are given on this answer sheet."

Also sign your name on the line provided and enter today's date (in numbers).

SIGNED:
(WRITE YOUR NAME AS IF SIGNING A BUSINESS LETTER)

DATE: _____ / _____ / _____
MO   DAY   YEAR

DO NOT MARK IN THIS AREA.

TEST FORM:

Reprinted by permission

171

SIDE 2

FORM

SEX
☐ MALE
☐ FEMALE

TEST BOOK SERIAL NUMBER

DATE OF BIRTH
/ /
MO DAY YEAR

SEAT NUMBER

Choose only one answer for each question. Carefully and completely fill in the oval corresponding to the answer you choose so that the letter inside the oval cannot be seen. Completely erase any other marks you may have made.

	CORRECT	WRONG	WRONG	WRONG	WRONG	WRONG
	Ⓐ	Ⓐ	Ⓐ	Ⓐ	Ⓐ	Ⓐ
	Ⓑ	Ⓑ	Ⓑ	Ⓑ	Ⓑ	Ⓑ
	●	Ⓒ	Ⓒ	Ⓧ	●	●
	Ⓓ	Ⓓ	Ⓓ	Ⓓ	Ⓓ	Ⓓ

NAME (Print)

FAMILY NAME (SURNAME)   GIVEN (FIRST) NAME   MIDDLE NAME

REGISTRATION NUMBER

SIGNATURE

SECTION 1

SECTION 2

SECTION 3

THIS IS A SAMPLE ANSWER SHEET

SCORE CANCELLATION

If you want to cancel your scores from this administration, complete A and B below. The scores will not be sent to you or your designated recipients, and they will be deleted from your permanent record.
To cancel your scores from this test administration, you must:

A. fill in both ovals here   and   B. sign your name in full below
   O – O

ONCE A SCORE IS CANCELED, IT CANNOT BE REINSTATED ON YOUR PERMANENT RECORD.

1R		2R		3R		TCS
1CS		2CS		3CS		E

FOR ETS USE ONLY

Reprinted by permission.

REGISTRATION NUMBER		TEST CENTER		TEST BOOK SERIAL NUMBER		TEST DATE

Begin your essay here. If you need more space, use the other side.

TOPIC

Q1381-07

DO NOT WRITE IN THIS AREA.

0   0   7   3   2   0   7

THIS IS A SAMPLE ANSWER SHEET

Reprinted by permission.

DO NOT WRITE BELOW THIS LINE. FOR ETS USE ONLY.

ORS

NO ○

OFF ○

TEST OF ENGLISH AS A FOREIGN LANGUAGE

THIS IS A SAMPLE ANSWER SHEET

SIDE 1

1. NAME: Print your name as it appears on your admission ticket. Using one box for each letter, first print your family name (surname); then your given name, and then your middle name. Leave one box blank between names. Then, below each box, fill in the oval that contains the same letter.

Use a No. 2 (H.B.) pencil only. Do not use ink. Be sure each mark is dark and completely fills the intended oval. Erase errors or stray marks completely.

2. REGISTRATION NUMBER

→ Start here

YOUR REGISTRATION NUMBER IS PRINTED TO THE RIGHT AND IS IN MACHINE READABLE FORM.

DO NOT RE-ENTER THE NUMBER HERE.

3. INSTITUTION AND DEPARTMENT CODES: Give the code numbers of the institutions and departments to which you want your official score report sent. Be sure to fill in the corresponding oval below each box.

INSTITUTION CODE / DEPT. CODE (repeated)

4. DO YOU PLAN TO STUDY FOR A DEGREE IN THE U.S.A. OR CANADA?
○ YES   ○ NO

5. REASON FOR TAKING TOEFL (FILL IN ONLY ONE OVAL)

○ 1. To enter a college or university as an undergraduate student.
○ 2. To enter a college or university as a graduate student.
○ 3. To enter a school other than a college or university.
○ 4. To become licensed to practice my profession in the U.S.A. or Canada.
○ 5. To demonstrate my proficiency in English to the company for which I work or expect to work.
○ 6. Other than the above (please specify)

6. NUMBER OF TIMES YOU HAVE TAKEN TOEFL BEFORE
○ NONE   ○ THREE
○ ONE   ○ FOUR OR MORE
○ TWO

7. CENTER (Print.)

COUNTRY   CITY   CENTER NUMBER

8. PLEASE PRINT IN BLOCK LETTERS YOUR NAME AND MAILING ADDRESS.

FAMILY NAME (SURNAME)   GIVEN (FIRST) NAME   MIDDLE NAME

STREET ADDRESS OR P.O. BOX NO

CITY   STATE OR PROVINCE

POSTAL OR ZIP CODE   COUNTRY

9. SIGNATURE AND DATE: Please copy the following statement in the space provided below; use handwriting.

"I hereby agree to the conditions set forth in the Bulletin of Information and affirm that I am the person whose name and address are given on this answer sheet."

Also sign your name on the line provided and enter today's date (in numbers).

SIGNED: _____ (WRITE YOUR NAME AS IF SIGNING A BUSINESS LETTER)

DATE: _____ / _____ / _____
      MO   DAY   YEAR

DO NOT MARK IN THIS AREA.

TEST FORM:

DO NOT WRITE IN THIS AREA.

0   2   1   5   2   3   5

175

SIDE 2

FORM

TEST BOOK SERIAL NUMBER

SEAT NUMBER

Choose only one answer for each question. Carefully and completely fill in the oval corresponding to the answer you choose so that the letter inside the oval cannot be seen. Completely erase any other marks you may have made. Choose only one answer for each question.

CORRECT	WRONG	WRONG	WRONG	WRONG

NAME (Print) _____
FAMILY NAME (SURNAME)   GIVEN (FIRST NAME)   MIDDLE NAME

SEX   ☐ MALE   ☐ FEMALE

DATE OF BIRTH   MO / DAY / YEAR

REGISTRATION NUMBER

SIGNATURE

SECTION 1

SECTION 2

SECTION 3

THIS IS A SAMPLE ONLY

SAMPLE

SCORE CANCELLATION

If you want to cancel your scores from this administration, complete A and B below. The scores will not be sent to you or your designated recipients, and they will be deleted from your permanent record. To cancel your scores from this test administration, you must:

A. fill in both ovals here   and B. sign your name in full below

○ — ○

ONCE A SCORE IS CANCELED, IT CANNOT BE REINSTATED ON YOUR PERMANENT RECORD.

1R	2R	3R	TCS	FOR ETS USE ONLY	F
1CS	2CS	3CS			

® **TOEFL ESSAY PAGE** **SIDE 3**

Begin your essay here. If you need more space, use the other side.

TOPIC [ ]

Q1381-07

177

0   0   7   3   2   0   7

SIDE 4
Continuation of essay

THIS IS A SAMPLE ANSWER SHEET

Reprinted by permission.

DO NOT WRITE BELOW THIS LINE. FOR ETS USE ONLY.

ORS

NO ◯

OFF ◯

178

TEST OF ENGLISH AS A FOREIGN LANGUAGE

SIDE 1

THIS IS A SAMPLE ANSWER SHEET

DO NOT WRITE IN THIS AREA.

0 2 1 5 2 3 5

Use a No. 2 (H.B.) pencil only. Do not use ink. Be sure each mark is dark and completely fills the intended oval. Erase errors or stray marks completely.

1. NAME: Print your name as it appears on your admission ticket, first print your family name (surname), then your given name, and then your middle name. Leave one box blank between names. Then, below each box, fill in the oval that contains the same letter.

2. REGISTRATION NUMBER

Start here

YOUR REGISTRATION NUMBER IS PRINTED TO THE RIGHT AND IS IN MACHINE READABLE FORM.

DO NOT RE-ENTER THE NUMBER HERE.

3. INSTITUTION AND DEPARTMENT CODES: Give the code numbers of the institutions and departments to which you want your official score report sent. Be sure to fill in the corresponding oval below each box.

INSTITUTION CODE | DEPT. CODE | INSTITUTION CODE | DEPT. CODE | INSTITUTION CODE | DEPT. CODE | INSTITUTION CODE | DEPT. CODE

4. DO YOU PLAN TO STUDY FOR A DEGREE IN THE U.S.A. OR CANADA?

○ YES   ○ NO

5. REASON FOR TAKING TOEFL (FILL IN ONLY ONE OVAL)

1. To enter a college or university as an undergraduate student.
2. To enter a college or university as a graduate student.
3. To enter a school other than a college or university.
4. To become licensed to practice my profession in the U.S.A. or Canada.
5. To demonstrate my proficiency in English to the company for which I work or expect to work.
6. Other than the above (please specify)

6. NUMBER OF TIMES YOU HAVE TAKEN TOEFL BEFORE

○ NONE   ○ THREE
○ ONE   ○ FOUR OR MORE
○ TWO

7. CENTER (Print.)

COUNTRY   CITY   CENTER NUMBER

8. PLEASE PRINT IN BLOCK LETTERS YOUR NAME AND MAILING ADDRESS.

FAMILY NAME (SURNAME)   GIVEN (FIRST) NAME   MIDDLE NAME

STREET ADDRESS OR P.O. BOX NO.

CITY   STATE OR PROVINCE

POSTAL OR ZIP CODE   COUNTRY

9. SIGNATURE AND DATE: Please copy the following statement in the space provided below; use handwriting.
"I hereby agree to the conditions set forth in the Bulletin of Information and affirm that I am the person whose name and address are given on this answer sheet."
Also sign your name on the line provided and enter today's date (in numbers).

SIGNED:
(WRITE YOUR NAME AS IF SIGNING A BUSINESS LETTER)

DATE: MO / DAY / YEAR

DO NOT MARK IN THIS AREA.

TEST FORM:

SIDE 2

FORM

SEX
☐ MALE
☐ FEMALE

TEST BOOK SERIAL NUMBER

DATE OF BIRTH

SEAT NUMBER

MO. / DAY / YEAR

Choose only one answer for each question. Carefully and completely fill in the oval corresponding to the answer you choose so that the letter inside the oval cannot be seen. Completely erase any other marks you may have made.

NAME (Print)

FAMILY NAME (SURNAME)   GIVEN (FIRST) NAME   MIDDLE NAME

REGISTRATION NUMBER

SIGNATURE

	CORRECT	WRONG	WRONG	WRONG	WRONG
A	Ⓐ	Ⓐ	Ⓐ	Ⓐ	Ⓐ
B	Ⓑ	Ⓑ	Ⓑ	Ⓑ	Ⓑ
	●	Ⓑ	⊗	⓪	ⓔ
D	Ⓓ	Ⓓ	Ⓓ	Ⓓ	Ⓓ

SECTION 1

SECTION 2

SECTION 3

THIS IS A SAMPLE ANSWER SHEET

SCORE CANCELLATION

If you want to cancel your scores from this administration, complete A and B below. The scores will not be sent to you or your designated recipients, and they will be deleted from your permanent record.
To cancel your scores from this test administration, you must:

A. fill in both ovals here   and   B. sign your name in full below

◯ – ◯

ONCE A SCORE IS CANCELED, IT CANNOT BE REINSTATED ON YOUR PERMANENT RECORD.

Reprinted by permission.

1R	2R	3R	
			E
1CS	2CS	3CS	
	TCS		

FOR ETS USE ONLY

180

REGISTRATION NUMBER		TEST CENTER		TEST BOOK SERIAL NUMBER		TEST DATE

Begin your essay here. If you need more space, use the other side.

TOPIC

DO NOT WRITE IN THIS AREA.

0   0   7   3   2   0   7

THIS IS A SAMPLE ANSWER SHEET

Reprinted by permission.

DO NOT WRITE BELOW THIS LINE. FOR ETS USE ONLY.

TEST OF ENGLISH AS A FOREIGN LANGUAGE

SIDE 1

THIS IS A SAMPLE ANSWER SHEET

1. NAME: Print your name as it appears on your admission ticket, first print your family name (surname), then your given name, and then your middle name. Leave one box blank between names. Then, below each box, fill in the oval that contains the same letter.

Use a No. 2 (H.B.) pencil only. Do not use ink. Be sure each mark is dark and completely fills the intended oval. Erase errors or stray marks completely.

2. REGISTRATION NUMBER
→ Start here

YOUR REGISTRATION NUMBER IS PRINTED TO THE RIGHT AND IS IN MACHINE READABLE FORM.

DO NOT RE-ENTER THE NUMBER HERE.

DO NOT WRITE IN THIS AREA.

0 2 1 5 2 3 5

3. INSTITUTION AND DEPARTMENT CODES: Give the code numbers of the institutions and departments to which you want your official score report sent. Be sure to fill in the corresponding oval below each box.

INSTITUTION CODE — DEPT CODE

4. DO YOU PLAN TO STUDY FOR A DEGREE IN THE U.S.A. OR CANADA?
○ YES   ○ NO

5. REASON FOR TAKING TOEFL. (FILL IN ONLY ONE OVAL.)

1. ○ To enter a college or university as an undergraduate student.
2. ○ To enter a college or university as a graduate student.
3. ○ To enter a school other than a college or university.
4. ○ To become licensed to practice my profession in the U.S.A. or Canada.
5. ○ To demonstrate my proficiency in English to the company for which I work or expect to work.
6. ○ Other than the above (please specify)

6. NUMBER OF TIMES YOU HAVE TAKEN TOEFL BEFORE
○ NONE   ○ THREE
○ ONE   ○ FOUR OR MORE
○ TWO

7. CENTER (Print.)

COUNTRY
CITY
CENTER NUMBER

8. PLEASE PRINT IN BLOCK LETTERS YOUR NAME AND MAILING ADDRESS.

FAMILY NAME (SURNAME)   GIVEN (FIRST) NAME   MIDDLE NAME

STREET ADDRESS OR P.O. BOX NO

CITY   STATE OR PROVINCE

POSTAL OR ZIP CODE   COUNTRY

9. SIGNATURE AND DATE: Please copy the following statement in the space provided below; use handwriting.

"I hereby agree to the conditions set forth in the Bulletin of Information and affirm that I am the person whose name and address are given on this answer sheet."

Also sign your name on the line provided and enter today's date (in numbers).

SIGNED: _____ (WRITE YOUR NAME AS IF SIGNING A BUSINESS LETTER)

DATE: ____ / ____ / ____
       MO   DAY   YEAR

DO NOT MARK IN THIS AREA.

TEST FORM.

183

SIDE 2

FORM

TEST BOOK SERIAL NUMBER

SEAT NUMBER

SEX	DATE OF BIRTH
☐ MALE ☐ FEMALE	MO / DAY / YEAR

Choose only one answer for each question. Carefully and completely fill in the oval corresponding to the answer you choose so that the letter inside the oval cannot be seen. Completely erase any other marks you may have made. Choose only one answer for each question.

CORRECT	WRONG	WRONG	WRONG	WRONG

NAME (Print) _____

FAMILY NAME (SURNAME)   GIVEN (FIRST NAME)   MIDDLE NAME

REGISTRATION NUMBER   **SIGNATURE**

THIS IS A SAMPLE ONLY

SECTION 1

1 Ⓐ Ⓑ Ⓒ Ⓓ
2 Ⓐ Ⓑ Ⓒ Ⓓ
3 Ⓐ Ⓑ Ⓒ Ⓓ
4 Ⓐ Ⓑ Ⓒ Ⓓ
5 Ⓐ Ⓑ Ⓒ Ⓓ
6 Ⓐ Ⓑ Ⓒ Ⓓ
7 Ⓐ Ⓑ Ⓒ Ⓓ
8 Ⓐ Ⓑ Ⓒ Ⓓ
9 Ⓐ Ⓑ Ⓒ Ⓓ
10 Ⓐ Ⓑ Ⓒ Ⓓ
11 Ⓐ Ⓑ Ⓒ Ⓓ
12 Ⓐ Ⓑ Ⓒ Ⓓ
13 Ⓐ Ⓑ Ⓒ Ⓓ
14 Ⓐ Ⓑ Ⓒ Ⓓ
15 Ⓐ Ⓑ Ⓒ Ⓓ
16 Ⓐ Ⓑ Ⓒ Ⓓ
17 Ⓐ Ⓑ Ⓒ Ⓓ
18 Ⓐ Ⓑ Ⓒ Ⓓ
19 Ⓐ Ⓑ Ⓒ Ⓓ
20 Ⓐ Ⓑ Ⓒ Ⓓ
21 Ⓐ Ⓑ Ⓒ Ⓓ
22 Ⓐ Ⓑ Ⓒ Ⓓ
23 Ⓐ Ⓑ Ⓒ Ⓓ
24 Ⓐ Ⓑ Ⓒ Ⓓ
25 Ⓐ Ⓑ Ⓒ Ⓓ
26 Ⓐ Ⓑ Ⓒ Ⓓ
27 Ⓐ Ⓑ Ⓒ Ⓓ
28 Ⓐ Ⓑ Ⓒ Ⓓ
29 Ⓐ Ⓑ Ⓒ Ⓓ
30 Ⓐ Ⓑ Ⓒ Ⓓ
31 Ⓐ Ⓑ Ⓒ Ⓓ
32 Ⓐ Ⓑ Ⓒ Ⓓ
33 Ⓐ Ⓑ Ⓒ Ⓓ
34 Ⓐ Ⓑ Ⓒ Ⓓ
35 Ⓐ Ⓑ Ⓒ Ⓓ
36 Ⓐ Ⓑ Ⓒ Ⓓ
37 Ⓐ Ⓑ Ⓒ Ⓓ
38 Ⓐ Ⓑ Ⓒ Ⓓ
39 Ⓐ Ⓑ Ⓒ Ⓓ
40 Ⓐ Ⓑ Ⓒ Ⓓ
41 Ⓐ Ⓑ Ⓒ Ⓓ
42 Ⓐ Ⓑ Ⓒ Ⓓ
43 Ⓐ Ⓑ Ⓒ Ⓓ
44 Ⓐ Ⓑ Ⓒ Ⓓ
45 Ⓐ Ⓑ Ⓒ Ⓓ
46 Ⓐ Ⓑ Ⓒ Ⓓ
47 Ⓐ Ⓑ Ⓒ Ⓓ
48 Ⓐ Ⓑ Ⓒ Ⓓ
49 Ⓐ Ⓑ Ⓒ Ⓓ
50 Ⓐ Ⓑ Ⓒ Ⓓ

SECTION 2

1 Ⓐ Ⓑ Ⓒ Ⓓ
2 Ⓐ Ⓑ Ⓒ Ⓓ
3 Ⓐ Ⓑ Ⓒ Ⓓ
4 Ⓐ Ⓑ Ⓒ Ⓓ
5 Ⓐ Ⓑ Ⓒ Ⓓ
6 Ⓐ Ⓑ Ⓒ Ⓓ
7 Ⓐ Ⓑ Ⓒ Ⓓ
8 Ⓐ Ⓑ Ⓒ Ⓓ
9 Ⓐ Ⓑ Ⓒ Ⓓ
10 Ⓐ Ⓑ Ⓒ Ⓓ
11 Ⓐ Ⓑ Ⓒ Ⓓ
12 Ⓐ Ⓑ Ⓒ Ⓓ
13 Ⓐ Ⓑ Ⓒ Ⓓ
14 Ⓐ Ⓑ Ⓒ Ⓓ
15 Ⓐ Ⓑ Ⓒ Ⓓ
16 Ⓐ Ⓑ Ⓒ Ⓓ
17 Ⓐ Ⓑ Ⓒ Ⓓ
18 Ⓐ Ⓑ Ⓒ Ⓓ
19 Ⓐ Ⓑ Ⓒ Ⓓ
20 Ⓐ Ⓑ Ⓒ Ⓓ
21 Ⓐ Ⓑ Ⓒ Ⓓ
22 Ⓐ Ⓑ Ⓒ Ⓓ
23 Ⓐ Ⓑ Ⓒ Ⓓ
24 Ⓐ Ⓑ Ⓒ Ⓓ
25 Ⓐ Ⓑ Ⓒ Ⓓ
26 Ⓐ Ⓑ Ⓒ Ⓓ
27 Ⓐ Ⓑ Ⓒ Ⓓ
28 Ⓐ Ⓑ Ⓒ Ⓓ
29 Ⓐ Ⓑ Ⓒ Ⓓ
30 Ⓐ Ⓑ Ⓒ Ⓓ
31 Ⓐ Ⓑ Ⓒ Ⓓ
32 Ⓐ Ⓑ Ⓒ Ⓓ
33 Ⓐ Ⓑ Ⓒ Ⓓ
34 Ⓐ Ⓑ Ⓒ Ⓓ
35 Ⓐ Ⓑ Ⓒ Ⓓ
36 Ⓐ Ⓑ Ⓒ Ⓓ
37 Ⓐ Ⓑ Ⓒ Ⓓ
38 Ⓐ Ⓑ Ⓒ Ⓓ
39 Ⓐ Ⓑ Ⓒ Ⓓ
40 Ⓐ Ⓑ Ⓒ Ⓓ

SECTION 3

1 Ⓐ Ⓑ Ⓒ Ⓓ   31 Ⓐ Ⓑ Ⓒ Ⓓ
2 Ⓐ Ⓑ Ⓒ Ⓓ   32 Ⓐ Ⓑ Ⓒ Ⓓ
3 Ⓐ Ⓑ Ⓒ Ⓓ   33 Ⓐ Ⓑ Ⓒ Ⓓ
4 Ⓐ Ⓑ Ⓒ Ⓓ   34 Ⓐ Ⓑ Ⓒ Ⓓ
5 Ⓐ Ⓑ Ⓒ Ⓓ   35 Ⓐ Ⓑ Ⓒ Ⓓ
6 Ⓐ Ⓑ Ⓒ Ⓓ   36 Ⓐ Ⓑ Ⓒ Ⓓ
7 Ⓐ Ⓑ Ⓒ Ⓓ   37 Ⓐ Ⓑ Ⓒ Ⓓ
8 Ⓐ Ⓑ Ⓒ Ⓓ   38 Ⓐ Ⓑ Ⓒ Ⓓ
9 ◯ ◯ ◯ ◯   39 Ⓐ Ⓑ Ⓒ Ⓓ
10 Ⓐ Ⓑ Ⓒ Ⓓ   40 Ⓐ Ⓑ Ⓒ Ⓓ
11 Ⓐ Ⓑ Ⓒ Ⓓ   41 Ⓐ Ⓑ Ⓒ Ⓓ
12 Ⓐ Ⓑ Ⓒ Ⓓ   42 Ⓐ Ⓑ Ⓒ Ⓓ
13 Ⓐ Ⓑ Ⓒ Ⓓ   43 Ⓐ Ⓑ Ⓒ Ⓓ
14 Ⓐ Ⓑ Ⓒ Ⓓ   44 Ⓐ Ⓑ Ⓒ Ⓓ
15 Ⓐ Ⓑ Ⓒ Ⓓ   45 Ⓐ Ⓑ Ⓒ Ⓓ
16 Ⓐ Ⓑ Ⓒ Ⓓ   46 Ⓐ Ⓑ Ⓒ Ⓓ
17 Ⓐ Ⓑ Ⓒ Ⓓ   47 Ⓐ Ⓑ Ⓒ Ⓓ
18 Ⓐ Ⓑ Ⓒ Ⓓ   48 Ⓐ Ⓑ Ⓒ Ⓓ
19 Ⓐ Ⓑ Ⓒ Ⓓ   49 Ⓐ Ⓑ Ⓒ Ⓓ
20 Ⓐ Ⓑ Ⓒ Ⓓ   50 Ⓐ Ⓑ Ⓒ Ⓓ
21 Ⓐ Ⓑ Ⓒ Ⓓ   51 Ⓐ Ⓑ Ⓒ Ⓓ
22 Ⓐ Ⓑ Ⓒ Ⓓ   52 Ⓐ Ⓑ Ⓒ Ⓓ
23 Ⓐ Ⓑ Ⓒ Ⓓ   53 Ⓐ Ⓑ Ⓒ Ⓓ
24 Ⓐ Ⓑ Ⓒ Ⓓ   54 Ⓐ Ⓑ Ⓒ Ⓓ
25 Ⓐ Ⓑ Ⓒ Ⓓ   55 Ⓐ Ⓑ Ⓒ Ⓓ
26 Ⓐ Ⓑ Ⓒ Ⓓ   56 Ⓐ Ⓑ Ⓒ Ⓓ
27 Ⓐ Ⓑ Ⓒ Ⓓ   57 Ⓐ Ⓑ Ⓒ Ⓓ
28 Ⓐ Ⓑ Ⓒ Ⓓ   58 Ⓐ Ⓑ Ⓒ Ⓓ
29 Ⓐ Ⓑ Ⓒ Ⓓ   59 Ⓐ Ⓑ Ⓒ Ⓓ
30 Ⓐ Ⓑ Ⓒ Ⓓ   60 Ⓐ Ⓑ Ⓒ Ⓓ

SAMPLE

SCORE CANCELLATION

If you want to cancel your scores from this administration, complete A and B below. The scores will not be sent to you or your designated recipients, and they will be deleted from your permanent record. To cancel your scores from this test administration, you must:

A. fill in both ovals here   and B. sign your name in full below

◯ — ◯

ONCE A SCORE IS CANCELED, IT CANNOT BE REINSTATED ON YOUR PERMANENT RECORD.

1R	2R	3R	TCS	FOR ETS USE ONLY	F
1CS	2CS	3CS			

REGISTRATION NUMBER		TEST CENTER		TEST BOOK SERIAL NUMBER		TEST DATE

Begin your essay here. If you need more space, use the other side.

TOPIC

Q1381-07

185

DO NOT WRITE IN THIS AREA.

0 0 7 3 2 0 7

THIS IS A SAMPLE ANSWER SHEET

Reprinted by permission.

DO NOT WRITE BELOW THIS LINE. FOR ETS USE ONLY.

ORS

NO ◯

OFF ◯